DYNAMIC INVESTING

DYNAMIC INVESTING

THE SYSTEM FOR AUTOMATIC PROFITS— NO MATTER WHICH WAY THE MARKET GOES

JEROME TUCCILLE

NAL BOOKS

NEW AMERICAN LIBRARY

TIMES MIRROR

NEW YORK AND SCARBOROUGH, ONTARIO

Published simultaneously in Canada by
The New American Library of Canada Limited

NAL BOOKS TRADEMARK REG. U.S. PAT. OFF. AND FOREIGN COUNTRIES
REGISTERED TRADEMARK—MARCA REGISTRADA
HECHO EN HARRISONBURG, VA. U.S.A.

SIGNET, SIGNET CLASSICS, MENTOR, PLUME, MERIDIAN and
NAL BOOKS are published *in the United States* by
The New American Library, Inc., 1633 Broadway, New York,
New York 10019, *in Canada* by
The New American Library of Canada Limited,
81 Mack Avenue, Scarborough, Ontario M1L 1M8

Designed by Julian Hamer

Library of Congress Cataloging in Publication Data

Tucille, Jerome.
Dynamic investing.

1. Investments. I. Title.
HG4521.T78   332.6'78   80-27956
ISBN 0-453-00398-2

First Printing, March, 1981

1 2 3 4 5 6 7 8 9

PRINTED IN THE UNITED STATES OF AMERICA

Contents

PART II

PART III

Introduction

By the time you finish this book you will know *exactly what to do with your money at all times*. Whether you are a sophisticated veteran with years of experience in various investment markets or an eager beginner, this book will provide you with an *automatic* program for becoming a winner in an increasingly turbulent financial climate.

The United States is a country where 7 percent inflation was once considered unacceptably high. A few short years ago a return of 8 or 9 percent a year on our money seemed desirable. The value of gold, platinum, silver, and other precious metals used to fluctuate a mere fifty cents or a dollar overnight, stock market cycles lasted six to nine months and longer, and it was possible to keep a bit ahead of inflation by utilizing relatively simple investment techniques.

Now the rules have suddenly been changed.

In the early months of 1980 inflation in the United States reached an unthinkable annualized rate of 18 percent. The prime lending rate to major corporations soared to an astronomical 20 percent. Treasury bills, the most conservative and risk-free investment of all, yielded as high as 16½ percent for three-month loans to the government. Think of that: the United States government had to pay 16½ percent interest to borrow money from its own citizens. There simply is no way that personal income, particularly income after taxes, can keep up with such devastating figures. Middle-class Americans, out of necessity, have grown more and more desperate to preserve what they have and build a solid financial foundation for the future.

In two of my earlier investment books I outlined a program designed to give the investor a return of 20 to 25 percent a year. *The Optimist's Guide to Making Money in the 1980's* offered a total stock market system complete with buy and sell ranges for recommended stocks. *Mind Over Money* discussed the psychology of fear and greed that governs the market, and presented a list of rules to help the investor stick to the basic program and avoid being sidetracked by fast-talking hustlers.

So far the program has worked *even better* than anticipated, providing an annual return of more than 30 percent. The record is public and available for anyone to scrutinize (a brief review will be presented in Chapter One of this book).

However, because of the South Americanization of the U.S. economy, stock market returns of 20 to 25 percent, or even 30 percent, are not enough when you consider that 50 percent or more of these short-term profits are taxed away by the government. A *net* return of 10 to 15 percent a year is perfectly splendid in a time of 7 percent inflation, the rate at the time I wrote those books. But it is no longer sufficient when inflation surges into the teens and, as is possible in the future, even higher.

While I am still optimistic about the United States' prospects through the 1980s, and about the ability of the stock market to keep giving us returns on the order of 20 to 25 percent a year, dramatic new changes are in order. As long as political considerations continue to determine our economic policies, we can expect inflationary swings and interest rate cycles to fluctuate wildly. The main danger now is that the plateaus are getting higher with each cycle. We started with 1 percent inflation and watched it go to 4 percent before bringing it down again. Then we allowed it to rise to 7 percent and considered it a job well done when we lowered it to 4 percent. In the early 1970s inflation shot up to a dizzying 13 percent and we were content to bring it back down to 5 percent. In 1980 we ran inflation up to 18 percent before slamming the brakes on. It remains to be seen just how far we can lower it without triggering a massive economic depression. If history is any guide, it is quite possible that the next upswing will carry us into the stratosphere; 25 to 30 percent inflation the next time around no longer sounds impossible.

Now consider what this means to your money. With a *mere 7* percent inflation rate the buying power of your dollars is cut in *half* every ten years, with 14 percent inflation it is halved every five years, and with 25 percent inflation the real value of your money is cut in half in *less than three years*. Imagine that. You have $20,000 and in less than three years you're worth only $10,000.

This new climate demands a *total* investment strategy, employing stocks, treasury bills, gold and silver, real estate, bonds, tax shelters, and other vehicles. This book will present that updated program in detail. And it is an *automatic* program so that the investor, by devoting just a few minutes a week to his or her money, will know exactly what to buy and what to sell at any given moment.

PART
I

1

Optimism Revisited

In *The Optimist's Guide to Making Money in the 1980's*, first published in December 1978, I recommended twelve stocks for growth, along with automatic signals for selling them. In my following book, *Mind Over Money*, I was able to write in the postscript, which was dated September 1979:

> Those following the rules . . . would have accumulated stocks in December, 1978, the last best buying opportunity to date, and would now be taking profits with part of their holdings and putting the proceeds into a money market fund, which is currently yielding over 10 percent.

Three weeks later the market crashed.

The twelve stocks in question had *all* moved higher—indeed, some had split and the new shares kept advancing to unprecedented highs—providing the investor with substantial profits beyond those I initially projected. After the Crash of '79 the stock market made another dramatic upswing, offering a new opportunity for taking profits before the breathtaking collapse that started in mid-February 1980.

Let's take a look now at these stocks along with their suggested purchase prices and the trigger prices at which they would have been automatically sold. Those investors unfamiliar with this system will have a new chance to see how a stock *buying and selling* program should be set up. The recommended stocks were:

	Suggested purchase price	Suggested selling strategy
Pittston Co.	24	In all cases, I
Aetna Life &	32	recommended selling
Casualty	(before the split)	some shares each time
Westinghouse	18	the stock moved up a
General Motors	60	few points, and buying
Levi Strauss	28	back shares when the
	(before the split)	stock declined to the
Avon	46	suggested purchase
Continental Oil	26	price or below.
Honeywell	43	
Allis-Chalmers	23	
Heublein	25	
Northwest Industries	52	
	(before the split)	
ASA Ltd.	20	

I suggested that the average investor select maybe four or five stocks from this list and set up a portfolio with them. The four I selected for a sample portfolio were Pittston, Aetna, Levi Strauss, and ASA, and the annual return to date has been better than 30 percent. To be fair, however, let's see how an extremely wealthy investor would have made out had he set up a portfolio with the entire list.

Pittston Co.

Transaction	Cost	Value of portfolio	Proceeds
Buy 400 PCO @ 24	$ 9,600	$9,600	
Buy 100 PCO @ 17	1,700	8,500	
Sell 100 PCO @ 24		9,600	$ 2,400
Sell 200 PCO @ 30		6,000	6,000
Buy 200 PCO @ 24	4,800	9,600	
Sell 200 PCO @ 30		6,000	6,000
Total cost	$16,100		$14,400
	Approximate dividends		960
	Total proceeds		$15,360

This would be the total activity so far in this stock. We have bought our initial shares, bought more when the stock declined, sold off shares as the stock moved up, bought more when the stock fell again, then sold for profits on the next advance. These transactions have given us a return of 32.67 percent to date, calculated in the following way. Total proceeds ($15,360) plus value of the portfolio ($6,000) give us a *total equity* of $21,360. Our total investment so far in this particular stock is $16,100, so our profit is $5,260. This is a return of 32.67 percent over about a two-year period. Now let's move on to the next stock.

Aetna Life & Casualty

Transaction	Cost	Value of portfolio	Proceeds
Buy 400 AET @ 32	$12,800	$12,800	
Sell 100 AET @ 36		10,800	$ 3,600
Sell 100 AET @ 41		8,200	4,100
3-for-2 split—we now own 300 shares.			
Sell 100 AET @ 32		6,400	3,200
Sell 100 AET @ 37		3,700	3,700
Total cost	$12,800		$14,600
	Approximate dividends		1,650
	Total proceeds		$16,250

Our total equity is now $19,950 and our total cost was $12,800, giving us a return to date of $7,150, or *56 percent* over a year and a half (we owned this stock for less time than we owned Pittston, since it did not fall to our suggested purchase price until several months after we bought the other stock). The next stock on our list is:

Westinghouse

Transaction	Cost	Value of portfolio	Proceeds
Buy 400 WX @ 18	$7,200	$7,200	
Sell 100 WX @ 22		6,600	$2,200
Sell 100 WX @ 26		5,200	2,600
Total cost	$7,200		$4,800
	Approximate dividends		630
	Total proceeds		$5,430

Total equity of $10,630 minus an investment of $7,200 gives us a
profit of $3,430, or 47.6 percent over a year and a half.

General Motors

Transaction	Cost	Value of portfolio	Proceeds
Buy 300 GM @ 60	$18,000	$18,000	
Sell 100 GM @ 65		13,000	$ 6,500
Buy 100 GM @ 60	6,000	18,000	
Sell 100 GM @ 65		13,000	6,500
Buy 100 GM @ 60	6,000	18,000	
Buy 100 GM @ 55	5,500	22,000	
Sell 100 GM @ 60		18,000	6,000
Sell 300 GM @ 65			19,500
Total cost	$35,500		$38,500
		Approximate dividends	3,600
		Total proceeds	$42,100

Total equity of $42,100 minus an investment of $35,500 leaves a
profit of $6,600, or 18.6 percent over two years. This is an unsat-
isfactory performance, and because of this and an impending
recession that threatened to hit the automobile industry harder
than any other segment of the economy, the best course was to
abandon our position in the stock entirely. In February 1980 there
was also some talk that GM might have to cut its dividend, which
would send the stock plummeting well below our original purchase price. In addition (as you will see in Chapter Three), when
short-term interest rates began to climb above 15 percent, this
was the signal to move cash out of the stock market into short-
term instruments such as treasury bills and money market funds.
This does not mean that we are finished forever with this particular stock. When yields on money market instruments begin to
fall precipitously and the Dow Jones Industrial Average, or DJIA,
seems to be leveling below the 800 mark, that is the time to start
thinking about acquiring more stocks again. At this point GM
might once again look like a good buy. More on this later, but
first let's continue with our list of stocks.

Levi Strauss

Transaction	Cost	Value of portfolio	Proceeds
Buy 400 LVI @ 28	$11,200	$11,200	
Sell 100 LVI @ 35		10,500	$ 3,500
Sell 100 LVI @ 42		8,400	4,200
Sell 100 LVI @ 50		5,000	5,000
2-for-1 split—we now own 200 shares.			
Sell 200 LVI @ 37			7,400
Total cost	$11,200		$20,100
	Approximate dividends		600
	Total proceeds		$20,700

Total equity of $20,700 minus an investment of $11,200 leaves us with a $9,500 profit and an 85 percent return for approximately two years. Here, too, it's time to get out of the stock entirely, although for different reasons than was the case with GM. After a run like this in such a relatively brief period of time, it is unrealistic to assume that the stock will keep on reaping such handsome profits. Also, after the two-for-one split the stock went so high that the yield dropped to about 3 percent. I would not buy the split stock unless it fell to somewhere in the high teens and, therefore, would not want to risk holding it at this lofty price—it simply has too far to fall in the event of a sustained market collapse. I would, however, consider buying it back if the dividend were increased to a point where the stock was once again yielding better than 6 percent and selling for less than six times earnings.

Avon

Transaction	Cost	Value of portfolio	Proceeds
Buy 300 AVP @ 46	$13,800	$13,800	
Sell 100 AVP @ 53		10,600	$ 5,300
Sell 100 AVP @ 60		6,000	6,000
Buy 100 AVP @ 46	4,600	9,200	
Sell 200 AVP @ 53			10,600
Total cost	$18,400		$21,900
	Approximate dividends		1,120
	Total proceeds		$23,020

Total equity of $23,020 less an investment of $18,400 equals a profit of $4,620, a 25.1 percent return over two years. Just prior to the Crash of '79 was when we moved this cash into the money market, but I would consider taking a new look at this stock whenever yields on short-term securities fall back down to the low teens.

Continental Oil (Conoco)

Transaction	Cost	Value of portfolio	Proceeds
Buy 400 CLL @ 26	$10,400	$10,400	
Sell 100 CLL @ 32		9,600	$ 3,200
Sell 100 CLL @ 40		8,000	4,000
Sell 100 CLL @ 48		4,800	4,800
Sell 100 CLL @ 56			5,600
Total cost	$10,400		$17,600
	Approximate dividends		880
	Total proceeds		$18,480

Total equity of $18,480 less an investment of $10,400 leaves us with a profit of $8,080. This is 77.7 percent return over a two-year period. Wouldn't it be wonderful if every stock just kept going up and up like Conoco and Levi Strauss, so that we could exhaust our position before a market collapse provided us with a new opportunity to start all over again?

Honeywell

Transaction	Cost	Value of portfolio	Proceeds
Buy 300 HON @ 43	$12,900	$12,900	
Sell 100 HON @ 50		10,000	$ 5,000
Sell 100 HON @ 62		6,200	6,200
Sell 100 HON @ 75			7,500
Total cost	$12,900		$18,700
	Approximate dividends		760
	Total proceeds		$19,460

Our profit here over a period of two years is $6,560 on an investment of $12,900, for a return of 50.9 percent. The big mistake here was selling the stock too soon, since Honeywell eventually went beyond $100 a share. However, I would rather lock in the profits I have than get too greedy and watch modest profits turn into long-term losses.

More people lose money by not selling on time than for any other single reason. No one has a crystal ball, and no one can consistently buy at rock bottom and sell at the final peak. Our basic strategy is to buy stocks when they are at the lower end of their trading cycles, usually when the DJIA is below 800, then to sell off a portion of our shares as stock prices advance during the next upswing in the market. It is true that we would have made more money on Levi Strauss and Conoco had we just bought and held and finally sold all our shares at once when the market peaked. But it is also true that we would have lost money on other stocks had we followed this strategy. On balance, over the long haul, you will do better if you settle for modest profits on the scale of 25 percent a year than you will by stretching your luck, letting your money run, and trying for the big kill. There is nothing wrong with taking a shot on a high-flying stock in hopes of a big score, but this type of gamble is for play money you can afford to lose, not for your serious money.

Allis-Chalmers

Transaction	Cost	Value of portfolio	Proceeds
Buy 400 AH @ 23	$ 9,200	$9,200	
Sell 100 AH @ 30		9,000	$ 3,000
Sell 100 AH @ 37		7,400	3,700
Buy 100 AH @ 26	2,600	7,800	
Sell 100 AH @ 29		5,800	2,900
Sell 100 AH @ 37		3,700	3,700
Total cost	$11,800		$13,300
	Approximate dividends		1,000
	Total proceeds		$14,300

Total equity of $18,000 after two years against an investment of $11,800 adds up to a profit of $6,200, a return of 52.5 percent.

We would have done better by not buying back shares at 26, but at that point the market seemed to be bottoming out and the stock leveling. Generally speaking, you are better off not buying above the suggested purchase price, but certain circumstances, such as a dividend increase or unusually higher earnings, could be sufficient reason to raise your figures a notch if you think the market is about to rally again soon. In this particular case I would consider repurchasing additional shares when the following three conditions are met: the stock falls to the 23–25 range, the DJIA is below 800, and yields on short-term instruments and money market funds start dropping sharply through the low teens.

Heublein

Transaction	Cost	Value of portfolio	Proceeds
Buy 400 HBL @ 25	$10,000	$10,000	
Sell 100 HBL @ 30		9,000	$ 3,000
Buy 100 HBL @ 25	2,500	10,000	
Sell 100 HBL @ 30		9,000	3,000
Buy 100 HBL @ 25	2,500	10,000	
Sell 100 HBL @ 31		9,300	3,100
Total cost	$15,000		$9,100
	Approximate dividends		1,000
	Total proceeds		$10,100

The pattern on this stock during the past two years has been so steady it's downright boring. From 25 to 30 or 32, down to 25, back up to 30, down to 25, back to 30 again. The only reason for staying with the stock is because I believe that one of these days Heublein will build up a head of steam and start rolling along like Levi Strauss or Honeywell. When this happens it would be good to have at least 100 shares in reserve to participate. As you can see from the above figures, a profit of $4,400 on a $15,000 investment is only a 29.3 percent return over two years. We would be much further ahead had we simply sold *all* our shares each time the stock hit 30, and bought them back at 25. If Heublein fails to push past 32 on the next sustained rally, I would then consider adopting this strategy.

Northwest Industries

Transaction	Cost	Value of portfolio	Proceeds
Buy 300 NWT @ 52	$15,600	$15,600	
2-for-1 split—we now own 600 shares.			
Sell 300 NWT @ 34		10,200	$10,200
Sell 100 NWT @ 36		7,200	3,600
Total cost	$15,600		$13,800
		Approximate dividends	800
		Total proceeds	$14,600

Total equity of $21,800 less our $15,600 investment gives us a $6,200 profit, for a 39.7 percent return in approximately one and a half years. The last stock on our list is a gold stock.

ASA Ltd.

Transaction	Cost	Value of portfolio	Proceeds
Buy 400 ASA @ 20	$8,000	$8,000	
Sell 100 ASA @ 26		7,800	$ 2,600
Sell 100 ASA @ 32		6,400	3,200
Sell 100 ASA @ 38		3,800	3,800
Sell 100 ASA @ 45			4,500
Total cost	$8,000		$14,100
		Approximate dividends	800
		Total proceeds	$14,900

In this case our stock took a long time to finally explode, after churning around near 20 for what seemed like an intolerable period. When gold took off in late 1979, ASA erupted like a volcano. Our return over about a two-year period is 86.3 percent. What first appeared to be the biggest dog in the portfolio wound up giving us the largest individual return, thanks to the rush to gold as a hedge against inflation.

After reviewing the preceding pages we can see that our stock buying and selling program has produced returns ranging from 18.6 to 86.3 percent over 18 to 24 months. The basic ingredients of this program are as follows:

1. Select a portfolio of good quality stocks that pay good dividends. The basic yield should be at least 6 percent.

2. Start buying these stocks when they are at the low end of their trading cycles for the past few years. The best time to buy stocks is after a major selling spree when the DJIA is below 800, after all the forced margin selling has hammered the market down, and after all the panic sellers have taken their losses and run for the hills with their tails between their legs.

3. If you fail to catch the bottom and your stocks decline another few points, don't be afraid to pick up some extra shares. This program is predicated on the assumption that the market will continue to survive and fluctuate, that the country will not be flushed down the tubes never to rise again, that Armageddon and the Final Reckoning are not imminent. If you believe otherwise —if you subscribe to the doomsday notion that all is lost, it's all over—you don't belong in the stock market in the first place. You belong in a cave with your shotgun, your dried figs and nuts, and your cache of gold coins (although I've never been able to figure out what good all the gold in the world would do you in these circumstances anyway; there would be no safe place to store it with all the banks shut down, and nothing to trade it for).

4. Start selling shares when the market advances again and your stocks start moving up. Avoid the temptation to move into more volatile issues that are the latest darlings of the hour, unless it is only to take a shot with some mad money you have lying around. Confine your serious dollars to this program. Remember, anything that triples in a fortnight will come shooting down like Halley's comet at the first sign of market weakness.

5. Stay off margin. Pay in full for your stocks. At today's rates interest charges will eat you alive.

6. Move more fully into a cash position when the DJIA gets up around 950. *Do* keep some shares in reserve, however, since one of these days the Dow index will finally explode through 1000 with conviction and you'll want to be able to participate when it does.

This is the strategy we have been relying on to date. As I mentioned earlier, though, serious changes are in order, because of the new rules the government has imposed on us, and this includes changes in our program. I fully expect the stock market program just outlined to keep providing us with hefty returns. (I did not take commissions into consideration, which would have shaved a couple of percentage points from our total. But, on the other hand, neither did I add in the interest our cash was earning in a money market fund while it sat there during lulls in the stock market. These rates passed 10 percent in 1979, and soared to 18 percent by spring 1980.) But the financial climate has grown far more turbulent than it was when I first established this strategy.

For this reason and a few others that I will go into later on, a major overhaul is in order. Let's take a close look now at the new conditions that have changed the rules for all of us.

2

New Rules for New Winners

THE RECESSION THAT WOULDN'T COME

History was made in the United States starting in the second half of 1979. The South Americanization of our economy was finally completed. The process had been in effect for fifteen years or longer, and it reached full bloom in the final year of the last decade.

It is easy to blame it all on the Carter administration, but the real culprit behind the inflation that ran rampant in this country through most of the 1970s was the war in Vietnam. The war cost us dearly both in money and in lost and ruined lives, but we avoided paying the financial tab for a long time afterward. Instead we forced our allies and trading partners to pay for much of it by making them accept inflated paper dollars for their goods and services. Here we were gobbling up all that oil, importing all those foreign automobiles and radios and television sets, and paying for it all with a veritable avalanche of paper dollars churned out by the money machine in Washington, D.C.

But sooner or later the bubble had to burst. It almost broke in the early 1970s, when Richard Nixon first imposed wage and price controls, then abruptly lifted them, sending prices surging into airless space. To use Milton Friedman's analogy, it was akin to turning the heat up under a pressure cooker while simultaneously clamping the lid down. When the lid was eventually lifted, all those bottled-up pressures, those price and wage increases that had artificially been suppressed, could do nothing but explode.

Gerald Ford inherited the mess in 1974 and, to his credit, he decided to do the politically unpopular thing and fight inflation fast and hard. By tightening up on monetary growth and vetoing some forty-odd bills that came across his desk in search of his signature, he managed to bring inflation back down from 13 percent to something under 5 percent in two years. The cost of doing all this was rising unemployment and recession and, of course, his job. It is difficult to say what hurt Ford most—his pardon of Nixon, his refusal to help New York City out of its financial jungle, or his Scrooge-like attitude toward the public purse; whatever it was, he lost a tight election to Jimmy Carter.

Jimmy Carter's first mistake upon entering office was to turn the heat back on under the pressure cooker too quickly. In past inflationary cycles, our economic experts had always brought inflation back down to 2 or 3 percent before refueling the economy again. Five percent inflation is a high platform to start jumping back up from. It is understandable for a new president to want to pep up the economy once he takes office, but with inflation still as high as 5 percent it was simply too early in the game to begin priming the pump.

Jimmy Carter had four years ahead of him to get the economy back in shape. Had he done the dirty work in the first year of his administration, he could have reduced inflation to a 2 or 3 percent level. To do this, he would have had to accept the fact that the economy would be sluggish for an extra six months or a year, but he could have afforded this political risk during the first half of his administration. Then, with inflation bottoming out around 2 percent or so, he could have slowly—the key word here is *slowly*—begun to rebuild the economy, so that it would have been in an upswing, with more people back working, in time for the 1980 presidential election.

But Jimmy Carter started his administration off on the wrong foot. The problem was not so much bad advice as it was conflicting advice. The president was constantly being sidetracked by the other point of view. This indecision and chronic vacillation was evidenced by the fact that he had two or more major advisers in every important area. Secretary of State Cyrus Vance and National Security Adviser Zbigniew Brzezinski pulled him in opposite directions in foreign policy and he tried to follow them both simultaneously. And a succession of economic advisers, from Robert Strauss to Alfred Kahn to W. Michael Blumenthal, gave him contradictory advice about how to run the economy. As a result, his policies changed from week to week as he administered his own special brand of electric shock treatment.

So Jimmy Carter got the economy off to a running start early on in his administration and, in so doing, sent inflation into a new upward spiral. As the economy grew more robust, inflation inched up past 7 percent. Then Carter announced that inflation was the number one enemy, and that he would soon do something about it. But inflation wouldn't quit and the president still did not do much about it. He said he would tighten up on monetary growth, but monetary aggregates kept growing at an alarming rate. He said he would curtail government spending, but the federal deficit still assumed gargantuan proportions. At this point inflation was up over 10 percent—and then up to 13—and if the president was going to do some of the unpopular things that are required to stop inflation in its tracks, instead of merely trying to jawbone it to death, he had to act soon, because another election year would soon be coming up.

Then an unexpected development occurred.

The time was early 1979, and the Arabs were pushing up the price of oil. Not merely raising it a little, the way a shopkeeper raises the price of bread two cents a loaf, but jacking it up in astronomical leaps and jumps. Now Jimmy Carter had a scapegoat.

The Arabs are causing inflation, he said.

But the vast majority of Americans knew that the Arabs could not have accounted for inflation's rush up into the low teens. Studies showed that the rising cost of energy, with its filter-down effect through so much of the world economy, was responsible for about 2 percent of the total, but that still left 11 percent unaccounted for.

Now it was the spring of 1979, inflation was getting worse, and the start of a new campaign year was less than nine months away. Carter insisted that the Arabs were primarily responsible for Latin American-style inflation in the United States, and that the American people were at least partially to blame because they overheated their homes and drove their cars too much. If we really wanted to knock inflation down a peg or two, all we had to do was insulate our houses, turn the lights off when we left a room, and walk down to the corner for a quart of milk instead of hopping in our cars.

Then came summer and the energy crunch was at least temporarily over; Americans were consuming less black gold, not out of the goodness of their hearts, but mainly because they couldn't afford the damned stuff anymore. But still inflation wouldn't go away.

W. Michael Blumenthal had failed to halt inflation when he was head of the Federal Reserve, and so had William Miller. Now Carter brought in a heavy gun to do the job, Paul Volcker. Volcker had a long-standing reputation as a no-nonsense, hard-money man.

Volcker's first act as chairman of the Fed was to tighten the screws on interest rates in order to curtail the growth in the nation's money supply. The dollar rallied briefly against European currencies, and it appeared that the inflationary spiral might finally be broken. A month went by, then two months, and the figures got worse instead of better. Volcker knocked interest rates up again. The prime rate was nearing *15 percent*—who would have believed it?—and mortgage money was now going for 13½ percent in some states.

Some dissenting economists were beginning to say that rising interest rates were, in themselves, a cause of inflation, driving up the cost of everything from buying a home to charging a restaurant meal on an American Express card. The idea was to *stop* people from borrowing in the first place, countered Volcker, by making it prohibitively expensive to buy on credit. Once we dry up consumer spending, he said, inflation will level off and start to fall.

The only problem with this theory was that inflation was already so high, 13 or 14 percent, that it still made sense to borrow money at 14 or even 18 percent, since the interest was deductible from income. The *real* cost of money to someone in a 50 percent tax bracket was only 7 or 8 percent after taxes, a considerable bargain when inflation is running in the teens. And, ironically, the federal government was pushing more and more people into higher tax brackets through its inflationary policies, making the act of borrowing money economically attractive to a larger segment of our society.

So the spiral continued at a dizzying pace, the figures growing worse from week to week, and Volcker kept knocking interest rates up a notch at a time. Dissenters in the United States said he was pushing rates up too far, while the Europeans said his plan wasn't working because he didn't push them high enough. Meanwhile, back in the White House, Jimmy Carter was beginning to worry about running for reelection with inflation hovering at 15 or 16 percent, mortgage money costing 16 percent (when you could get financing at all), and the cost of money skyrocketing in general.

Carter was hoping for an early recession. He was hoping for one so badly that he sent all his economic advisers out into the hinterlands to inform the American people that a recession had either just begun or was surely just about to. There are several important political reasons why any president in Carter's shoes would have wanted a recession immediately instead of later on.

First of all, we had to have a recession sooner or later, since this is the only way that economists so far have been able to end an inflationary spiral.

Second, since a recession was coming, it would be better to get it started in 1979 and over with by mid-1980, so that good times could arrive again by the day of the election.

Third, an early recession would signal the beginning of the end of this latest inflationary cycle. This would mean that the Fed could start bringing interest rates back down again, which is a more pleasing state of affairs to a greater number of people.

Jimmy Carter, and any incumbent president for that matter, would prefer to take to the hustings with inflation and interest rates on the way down rather than up. But Carter went wrong by heating things up too quickly at the outset, and he put himself in the curious position of having to put a damper on his *own* artificially induced, ill-timed prosperity. His timing could not have been worse had the entire scenario been laid out for him by the Republican party.

Despite all the talk of recession, despite all the predictions by Carter's experts, the economy refused to cooperate. Try as they might, no one could spot a recession anywhere. The boom times simply refused to go away. The economy roared ahead like a drunk on a binge, people spent money as though they couldn't get rid of it fast enough, and inflation kept on inching up.

THE CRASH OF '79

All this was wreaking havoc on the American stock market. The market had been in a long-term "bear" cycle since 1968, after having peaked a little over 1000 on the Dow. Following the crash of 1974, which saw the DJIA plunge below the 600 mark, the market perked up a bit and has fluctuated in a rather narrow trading band between 750 and 1000 ever since. In 1968 dollars, the DJIA at 900 today translates into something less than 300. A pretty dismal performance, to say the least.

As we approached the fall of 1979 the stock market was moving up at a pretty good pace, with the Dow close to 900. Stockbrokers were happy, because business was relatively good, and so were their customers, whose stocks were moving up. But several warning signs started to appear, sounding a note of caution amid all this euphoria. Some of these signs were based in economic reality and some were psychological.

As far as reality was concerned, history was being made in a sense: the stock market was going up in the face of rising interest rates, which ordinarily would have put a damper on the market. When interest rates go up people usually pull money out of the stock market and move it into bonds, utilities, preferred stocks, or long-term deposits in banks to take advantage of the high rate of return. The fact that people were *not* doing this in the early fall of 1979 could only mean that no one truly believed that a recession had taken hold. In other words, investors expected interest rates to move higher still, since they also believed inflation was out of control.

Another element of reality that was history-making in a way was that the stock market was rising *at the same time* that gold was flying to unprecedented heights. In the past, gold and stocks have traditionally fluctuated *counter* to each other. People have always viewed gold as a hedge against inflation. Inflation means higher interest rates, which is good for gold and bad for the stock market. But here they were, gold and stocks, both flying higher simultaneously. Something weird was going on.

Psychologically, a great dark cloud began to drift over the stock market as we approached the fiftieth anniversary of the Crash of '29. This impending anniversary date was bad enough, but what made it worse was the fact that the media simply would not stop talking about it. Every time we turned on the television someone was reminding us that we were rapidly approaching the fiftieth anniversary of the Big Crash. Newspapers gave this approaching event front-page coverage. The Big Countdown had begun. Only 28 days left to the fiftieth anniversary of the Crash of '29. Only 22 days left to go. Several books hit the stores at once to provide us with the grisly history of Black Thursday.

Here it was, early October, 1979 and the warning signs were multiplying every day. Rising interest rates, rising gold prices, the fiftieth anniversary of the greatest financial disaster in history—and stock prices were still advancing. It was not a rally to be trusted. It was a time to lighten up a bit and convert stocks into cash, just to be on the safe side. There were too many contradictions at work. How long could all this craziness last, anyway? New rules seemed to be governing the marketplace.

Finally, the inevitable happened: the stock market crashed with a resounding bang. It didn't merely come down the way it usually does after a run-up, when the profit-taking sets in. In an ordinary sell-off resulting from profit-taking, you have time to get out without being hurt too badly. This time, however, the market suddenly lost wind and collapsed. On October 8, 1979, the stock market dropped 14 points on volume totaling 35 million shares. The following day it sank 27 points on 50 million shares. The panic was on: "Out, out, I want out! Get me out before I lose all my money!" One day later, October 10, all hell broke lose. Bedlam was never like this. On record high volume of 82 million shares, the market dove 25 points before rallying a bit to end the day down 8. The next day the market was like a yo-yo: up 2 on the opening, down 12, up 3, down 4 on lower volume. On the big day, October 24, the fiftieth anniversary of Black Thursday, 1929, the market was quiet. Volume was drying up and most of the carnage and bloodletting had already taken place. The stock market had given up over 100 points in the space of a couple of weeks. Some people, those who had bought stocks heavily on margin, were totally wiped out. Those with cash positions, those who paid in full for their stocks, saw their net worth drop 30 percent or more. But at least they owned their stocks outright; they could afford to hold and wait for the next market rally to make them whole again.

Meanwhile, gold was flying to the moon—to $600, $700, $800 an ounce. Silver, too—$35, $40, $50 an ounce. Things really didn't change after all.

THE END OF THE BOND MARKET

As bad as things were for the stock market, new rules were also affecting the fixed-income market, particularly bonds and utility stocks. In past years bonds, utility stocks, preferred stocks, anything people bought for income and safety, fluctuated moderately as interest rates went up and down a bit with inflation.

If you bought a bond when prevailing yields were in the neighborhood of 8 percent and a year or two later yields rose to 9 percent or so as inflation grew a bit worse, you might see the value of your bond fall 10 or 15 percent to reflect higher rates of interest. Annoying, to say the least, but not a major disaster. You knew that if you waited a while longer, interest rates would eventually fall and your bonds would be back up to par or maybe to a premium. Investors were willing to accept these moderate fluctuations in return for the steady income on good-quality bonds. Retired people in particular and others who simply did not want to lose any sleep over stock market gyrations bought their bonds, collected the interest, and didn't worry too much about the value of the bonds at any given moment.

The same thing was true for preferred stocks and utilities. Though not quite as safe as most bonds, the income from these investments was reasonably secure and their price movements were moderate.

But suddenly the rules changed for all of us in late 1979. Inflation was continuing to mount—16 percent, 17 percent, my God, the country was becoming a banana republic. Gold roared ahead to well over $800 an ounce, and Volcker kept on tightening the interest rate screws. The prime hit 17 percent, then 18 percent, and some analysts were saying 20 percent was not unthinkable.

Still inflation refused to come down, and Jimmy Carter would soon be entering an election year without his recession, and *with* the economy totally out of control. Just as things looked bleakest, just when it looked as though he could not possibly be reelected, two events on the international scene helped him out enormously. One was the seizure of American hostages in Iran, and the other was the Russian invasion of Afghanistan. Now Carter was too busy with foreign policy to talk about inflation. He was too preoccupied to even leave the White House and campaign.

In December 1979 people started to quietly buy stocks again. It appeared to many that interest rates had finally peaked, that inflation might be leveling off at an annualized rate of 18 percent, and that the long-awaited recession might have taken hold.

Also, the bond and fixed-income market was a shambles, with portfolio values off as much as 40 percent from their levels of only three or four years earlier. Incredible, but true: somebody who bought, say, $100,000 worth of high-grade bonds in 1976 was now worth only about $60,000. The bond market was fading out of sight. In some instances you could not even find a market for your bonds if you wanted to take your losses and get out. The same was true of common utility stocks and preferreds. Forty percent losses—a tragedy. A seemingly conservative investment of a few years back turned out to be a disaster. You might as well have taken your hundred thousand and shot craps.

The first six weeks of 1980 were boom times once again for the stock market. Brokers made half a year's pay in the first month of the year. The market started to roll in early January as people moved cash out of the banks, out of their bonds and so-called safe investments, and poured it into the stock market in anticipation of lower interest rates just ahead. Gold and silver were also falling apart, after peaking at $875 and $50 an ounce respectively. Many believed that a recession had already started a couple of months earlier, and the market almost always bottoms out two or three months into a recession. Led by the big oil stocks and the defense stocks (investors bought stocks like Boeing, General Dynamics, and Northrop in anticipation of increased defense spending), the DJIA pushed back up over 900 by the middle of February.

But once again warning signs began to appear on the horizon. Had we or had we not entered a recession? If we had, why wasn't inflation coming down the way it was supposed to? And why was the money supply still rising at a double-digit rate when interest rates were so high? The newest figures for inflation revealed it to be around 18 percent, even 20 percent in some parts of the country. Granted, you can't go entirely by weekly figures; there has to be a time lag. But there ought to have been some sign that the inflationary cycle had been broken or at least slowed.

Here it was, mid-February 1980, and Jimmy Carter could not afford to waste another minute. He needed an economic slump as soon as possible to break the back of inflation, and he needed one that would end before the November election.

With interest rates already at a record-high level after a series of quarter-point jumps over the past eight months, Volcker, with Carter's blessings, decided to tighten the screws all the way. No more halfhearted measures. The prime lending rate was bumped up a full point to 19 percent and then, a few days later, up another point to an even 20 percent. The magic level had been reached: a 20 percent prime. Just how high could it finally go—22 percent? 25? Was the unthinkable possible?

The reaction from investors was immediate. "We are not in a recession after all! Inflation is not coming down!" was the cry on Wall Street. Yields on treasury bills and six-month deposits were zooming, with 12, 13, 14 percent yields on absolutely safe short-term paper, and these returns would soon climb to 18 percent. "And here I am in the stock market with these kinds of yields available *without taking risk*. I've got my money in the wrong place!" said the stock investor.

The panic selling commenced once again, for the second time in four months. This time around the collapse was even worse than the October bloodbath. During the first ten days of this selling spree, the market lost 100 points, all the way back down to 800 on the Dow, after having peaked at 905. The selling continued from mid-February into March. And then, on March 27, just when it looked as though the market might be leveling in preparation for another upswing, a new disaster struck. The silver market collapsed after some heavy speculating by Nelson Bunker Hunt and Herbert Hunt, the sons of deceased oil billionaire H. L. Hunt, drove the price up as high as $50 an ounce.

A collapse in silver, as well as a collapse in gold, would not in itself have spelled trouble for the stock market. If anything, it would ordinarily have been bullish for stocks, for the reasons discussed a bit earlier. But this one had a different twist to it.

The breathtaking drop in silver, with the resulting margin calls amounting to hundreds of millions of dollars, threatened, for one harrowing hour, to sink the prestigious brokerage firm of Bache Halsey Stuart Shields, one of the largest in the country. The news went out over the Dow Jones newswire and hit the market like a shockwave. On rocketing selling volume the DJIA collapsed 27 points between 3:00 p.m. and 3:30, then abruptly changed course and roared back up 25 by the closing gong at 4:00 p.m. It was one of the most spectacular days in stock market history. One stock alone, Mobil Oil, was down 6 points at 3:30 and a half hour later ended the day up 3. The following day it was revealed that Bache would survive and so, apparently, would the market, as it has throughout its sometimes placid and sometimes rocky history. But it has become more and more of a game for those with nerves of steel, stomachs of cast iron, and sufficient agility to move in and out of different markets quickly as soon as certain signals, which we will discuss shortly, are sounded.

In April 1980 the prime rate peaked at 20 percent and was subsequently lowered. Yields on treasury bills fell dramatically in a matter of weeks, from a high of 16½ percent to below 8 percent; a recession, it appeared, had finally taken hold. Whether we were in a recession or not depended, of course, on the industry you worked in. Automobile workers and homebuilders were faced with a major depression; others did not feel the pinch until a bit later. Remember the grim old joke that used to make the rounds—What's the difference between a recession and a depression? When *you're* out of work it's a recession; when *I'm* out of work it's a depression.

A NEW ERA BEGINS

These new rules have made life a bit more complicated for all of us. They can be summed up as follows:

1. No longer can we count on inflation to remain under 10 percent. Incredible as it seemed a few years ago, we have already experienced double that figure in the United States, which means that the world in general has lost much of its remaining stability.

2. We have entered a new era of interest rates. Yields of 8 or 9 percent, attractive only a few years ago, are now puny and unacceptable.

3. The bond market and the fixed-income market in general has been irreparably damaged. These securities can still be bought, but only for trading purposes. Anyone who buys and holds with no intent to sell does so at his or her own peril.

4. There are no conservative investments left anymore. The entire concept of conservative, aggressive, and speculative investments has been rendered obsolete. Everything is speculative from this point on except for short-term instruments that are really just another form of interest-producing cash.

5. Stock market swings have gotten choppier, the cycles shorter. Full cycles can be accomplished in days and weeks today, whereas months and even years were required in the past. As a result, changes in our stock program outlined earlier are in order.

6. Whether we like it or not, the new rules have forced all of

us to become traders. No one can afford to hang around too long in any one market, and this includes the proverbial old lady in tennis shoes with her beloved portfolio of bonds and, of course, a few shares of AT&T stock.

7. Since profit-taking must be done on a short-term basis from now on, we must all become a bit more familiar with the tax laws. Anyone waiting for a long-term holding period, now a year and a day, to take profits must be willing to see his short-term profits turn into long-term losses. The question to ask is, "Which do I prefer? Paying taxes on short-term profits, or taking the time to learn how to shelter them—or watching these profits become irretrievable long-term losses?"

8. Shelter is now the name of the game—tax shelter. We must all live and breathe tax shelter. Anyone who fails to take the proper measures to shelter income and profits is only cheating himself.

9. While I am still optimistic that the United States will survive and prosper through the 1980s and beyond, we must accept the fact that the powers that be have let the game get out of control. They have manipulated us from one cycle to the next for political reasons, but as life has grown more and more complicated they have become less able to fine-tune the economy the way they used to.

Inflation, unfortunately, is going to be with us indefinitely, because the government wants it that way. Government is the only institution in the country to benefit from inflation, since, by pushing people into higher and higher tax brackets without any real increase in their buying power, government is increasing its own cash flow.

Simple inflation was bad enough, but now we must all be concerned about the specter of out-of-control inflation sometime in the future. It may come to pass that we will not have to grapple with 25 or 30 percent inflation the next time around, but we should all be prepared to deal with it in case we do.

What exactly do we do to make these new rules work for us? What do we buy or sell? When? These questions will be answered in the next chapter.

3

How to Make New Investment Profits—Automatically

In the years ahead there will be a time to be in the stock market, a time to be in gold, a time to be in short-term paper such as treasury bills and money market funds, and a time to be in bonds for trading profits.

The stock program I outlined in Chapter One is designed to generate a return of 20 to 25 percent a year and, so far, it has proved itself capable of doing that and better. However, it is *unrealistic* to expect that you will be able to do better than this consistently. You may get lucky from time to time and wind up with an extraordinarily successful year, but over the long haul the law of averages will catch up with you, the cycles will even out, and you will find it impossible to maintain the record.

Anyone who claims he can show you how to do better than this, on average, over a reasonable period of time is either a con artist or else God is telling him the future. If you are content to achieve the kinds of returns in the stock market we have been discussing, it is possible to do so with a disciplined program. But if greed gets the best of you, you are destined to become a loser. Forget about making the big score in the stock market unless you don't mind risking everything you have and going for broke. If you are built this way, then go ahead and do it. I personally know a number of people who are not rich but who, nevertheless, do not mind sinking $30,000 and $40,000 into the riskiest stocks imaginable in hopes of finding one that will become another Resorts International and make them rich. These are invariably the same types who can run off to Las Vegas and risk the same amount in craps without losing sleep over it.

This kind of playing, however, is not for me. I don't mind taking a shot once in a while with small amounts of cash, but I don't like to risk serious money on anything less than quality stocks. I continue to believe that my method of buying and selling stocks is best over the long term, especially for the average investor who can't sit around watching the tape all day long.

Over the years I have had many arguments with technicians and tape readers who claim they can do better by simply picking stocks that are moving right off the tape, and trading them for a quick point or two. But after seeing this system in action for quite some time and even experimenting with it myself in a small way, I have come to the conclusion that the major beneficiaries are the stockbrokers who rake in all the quick commissions. I have yet to meet a tape reader who has grown wealthy trading in this fashion, and some of the best ones I've known, who have been at it for twenty-five years and longer, still work for a living to pay their bills.

Besides, anyone who does not have the time to sit in a broker's office all day long following the action cannot trade stocks in this fashion. Most people have to rely on fundamentals in order to select their stocks. They are too busy to spend so much time watching their investments.

THE NEW PROGRAM

Because of the increased turbulence in the markets, and because of the incredibly high level inflation and interest rates have recently attained, I am changing the basic program as follows:

1. **Never buy stocks when the yields on risk-free, short-term instruments are higher than 12 or 13 percent.** The extra risk you have to assume to get a higher rate of return with stocks is not worth taking. Why gamble to make 20 percent before taxes when you can get 13 percent or better with treasury bills (for example) and get a tax break on the interest, since it is not subject to state or city income taxes? The risk-reward ratio does not warrant taking the chance. Also, with money market rates so high, other investors will also be keeping their money in treasury bills and money market funds, which means that the stock market is just going to sit there until short-term rates come down. Under these circumstances any stocks you buy will take quite some time to get moving.

The best time to buy stocks prior to the crash of March 1980 was in December 1979, following the big sell-off in October. The best time to sell those stocks for profits was in February 1980, when the Dow peaked a little above the 900 mark.

In the spring of 1980 the DJIA settled around 770, after having fallen as low as 739 in March. Under normal circumstances, I would have started accumulating stocks in a big way as soon as it looked as though the panic selling and margin calls were over. But unlike in December 1979, this time I held back.

Why?

Because treasury bills were still offering 12 percent for three-month loans to the government, and money market funds were paying anywhere from 14 to 18 percent for day-to-day money. It is extremely difficult to get a stock market rally going as long as people can get this kind of a return without taking any risk.

It did seem, however, that interest rates were coming down for real. The prime rate was reduced to 19 percent, short-term rates were slipping from week to week, and if this continued it would not be long before investors started moving money back into the stock market again.

I decided to acquire some stocks cautiously, but one thing bothered me more than anything else: inflation gave no sign of letting up. It still hovered at an annualized 18 percent level. The first sign that there was a break in inflation would trigger a strong rally, since it meant that interest rates and, consequently, yields on money market instruments would come down even faster.

When this happened, it would once again be time to *start buying stocks* heavily. If, on the other hand, inflation remained stubbornly high or moved even higher, then all bets would be off. The Fed would continue to maintain tight-money policies and might even push interest rates back up again. Short-term yields would rise and this would mean further trouble for the stock market for quite a bit longer.

2. **The best time to buy stocks is still when the DJIA is under 800,** assuming that yields on money market instruments have fallen below 12 or 13 percent. At that point it is worth assuming some risk to get the substantially higher return available in the stock market. If the DJIA ever does rally significantly beyond 1000 (and I believe that one day soon it most likely will) and stay there for a while, then I would update my buy signal at that time (see Part II). But for the moment 800 or lower, the market's bottoming area for the past few years, is my buying zone.

3. Stick to the kinds of stocks I mentioned in Chapter One: household names paying good dividends and selling for under six times earnings. (A complete list of recommendations appears in Part III.)

4. Unlike the old program, I am now suggesting that you sell off larger portions of stock as it advances in a market rally. For example, if I owned 500 shares of RCA at $20 a share and it moves up to 25, right now I would be inclined to sell 200 or 300 shares, instead of only 100 as in the past. If it runs up to 30 I would sell off more shares and keep 100 shares in reserve in order to participate if the stock should keep on moving to 40 or beyond. By adopting this strategy in place of the old one, you will be more fully in a cash position when the market peaks at 900 or 950 or maybe even 1000 again. You will then be about 80 percent out of the market and back into something else before all the new panic selling begins. You may even decide to dump your last 100 shares on the way down if it looks as though your stock may fall back to your original purchase price. Because the market has grown more volatile over the past couple of years, you will have to be nimbler and quicker to get out at the first sign of weakness.

More and more analysts have been talking about stocks as the new hedge against inflation for the 1980s. With real estate and gold already so high, the argument goes, stocks will once again return to favor.

It is rather refreshing to hear this, since I said essentially the same thing in 1978 in *The Optimist's Guide to Making Money in the 1980's*. But when too many people start saying the same thing, I begin to get a little nervous.

No one will be happier than I if the stock market starts to take off and just keeps on rolling nonstop until the DJIA hits 1500. We are way overdue for a long-term bull market, since the market is down considerably from its peak in 1968. At this time, however, I would rather move in and out for short-term profits to maximize my current return. If the market does explode beyond the trading range it has been moving in for the past few years, I will still have some shares in my portfolio that will enable me to participate. This hit-and-run strategy is better suited for the choppy and violent markets we have today.

MONEY MARKET INSTRUMENTS

The two best times to put money into short-term paper such as treasury bills and money market funds are, first of all, when you are taking profits in stocks and have large cash reserves on hand and, second, as I said before, when yields are moving back up through the low teens.

For the uninitiated, money market instruments are debt securities maturing within a year. These include treasury bills, bankers' acceptances, certificates of deposit, and commercial paper. Putting it another way, when you lend money to the federal government, a bank, or a corporation for less than a year, you are participating in the money market.

For most people, the three most popular ways to invest in the money market are treasury bills, money market funds, and six-month certificates of deposit (CDs) in a bank. Of these three, the interest on treasury bills is the only income that is exempt from state and local taxes.

Every Monday the federal government auctions off three-month and six-month bills. You need a minimum of $10,000 to subscribe to T-bills, and multiples of $5,000 above this figure. The easiest way to subscribe is by calling up your broker and telling him to put you into the Monday auction for whatever amount you want to invest. For this service he will charge you a $25 commission, whether you are investing $10,000 or $1 million. If you want to save the $25, you have the option of standing in line at a federal reserve bank for a couple of hours. Either way, you will not know ahead of time exactly what rate of interest you will be getting for your money, and you have to be willing to accept the going rate for the week. Your only guide is the previous week's rate, although it has been known to fluctuate by as much as a percentage point a week.

T-bills are the best deal in the money market since, besides the tax exemption on the interest, they are sold on a discounted basis. This means you are getting your *interest up front*. For example, let's assume you want to subscribe to $10,000 worth of three-month bills at next Monday's auction. Instead of putting up $10,000 now and collecting your interest later on, as is the case with bank certificates, you pay only $9,600 or $9,700 now, say, depending on the interest rate, and get $10,000 back when the bills mature. And you not only have your interest money *now,* but you are getting even more out of the deal, because the $300 or $400 interest you are receiving is a return on an investment of only $9,700, not $10,000 as with the bank certificates.

Interest up front; exemption from state and local taxes; discounted interest rather than a full $10,000 investment; full backing by the federal government: these are four reasons why treasury bills are far superior to bank CDs as a money market investment.

For *liquid* cash, that is, money you don't want to tie up for even three months, money market funds are the best bet around. These are no-load (no commission) mutual funds comprising a portfolio of money market instruments. There are many around and essentially they work like this. A major brokerage firm goes out into the market and buys a huge amount of short-term paper. Some of these portfolios contain T-bills and some don't, and some have higher-grade commercial paper and bank certificates than others, so there is a difference in quality. By and large, however, if you are dealing with a reputable firm the risk is minimal at most. This brokerage firm—let's call it Bull, Banks, Forbes & Trotsky—then sells shares in the portfolio to the investing public. You invest, say, $5,000 and you now own 5,000 shares in the portfolio, the value of which is maintained at $1 a share.

Strictly speaking, your shares do fluctuate with interest rates, but the managers of these funds will move interest money into the shares if they have to in order to maintain the $1 value. The interest from these securities compounds in the portfolio so that for all intents and purposes your money is working for you every day. You have what amounts to a day-to-day savings account with interest accruing daily, and no penalty for withdrawal. In addition, many of these funds issue checkbooks as well, which gives you a savings and checking-account system all in one.

Unlike bank accounts, money market funds are not backed by the Federal Deposit Insurance Corporations or FDIC. But in my opinion FDIC is a bit of a hoax in the first place, since it does not have nearly enough money on hand to guarantee all the money in deposit at the nation's banks. The whole system is predicated on the assumption that there will not be a run on the banks. If there were, if everyone lined up at the teller's windows tomorrow morning demanding cash, the banks would have no choice but to declare an indefinite bank holiday. The money, quite simply, is not on hand, and FDIC does not have enough legal tender at its disposal to pay off more than $1 out of $100 on deposit. Some banks, as a matter of fact, came pretty close to declaring something of a holiday when they announced, in the winter of 1980, that they would no longer redeem long-term deposits prematurely. They were responding to the fact that all the people who had put money into four-year and seven-year certificates a year or two earlier suddenly wanted to redeem them early, to take advantage of the soaring short-term rates of late 1979 and early 1980. Well, the banks got very uppity about this (even though according to the original terms of the deposit you were supposed to be able to redeem early if you were willing to pay a penalty), and in many cases they refused to let you have your money unless you agreed to roll it into short-term deposits at *their* banks.

So much for bank safety and risk-free security. Accept the fact that there is no such thing as absolute security, that we do not live in a risk-free environment, that there is an element of risk in everything we do, and act accordingly. Every transaction, every breath we take, involves a degree of risk, and there's no point worrying about events that are beyond our control.

So when yields on money market instruments start inching up toward 12 percent, when the DJIA has rallied beyond 900, it is time to start thinking about moving some money out of the stock market and into short-term paper. *Everybody else* will be thinking pretty much the same thing fairly soon, and that means there is no way the market will be able to sustain a further advance.

As you sell off shares of stock, put your cash into a money market fund. If you have large amounts of cash, keep some liquid in the fund and move larger amounts into treasury bills. If interest rates are moving up, subscribe to the *three-month* bills. This way you will get your cash back in a shorter period of time and can then roll it over into a new bill at a higher interest rate. At the end of the cycle, when rates are starting to come *down,* subscribe to the *six-month* bills. This way you will be locking in a relatively high rate of interest for a longer period of time while interest rates are declining. As short-term interest rates start dropping through the low teens, and if the stock market has sold off to a point where the DJIA is now below 800, start thinking about moving your cash back into the *stock market* again.

In the old days—three or four years ago—these cycles used to take years to work themselves out. The cycles were more gradual and the swings more gentle than they are now. Peaks and valleys were spaced pretty far apart.

Today this has changed, probably for good. The markets have grown violent. Peaks and valleys from one market to another are sometimes only weeks apart, particularly in the stock and precious metals markets. Interest rate cycles still take longer to complete themselves, but there are more secondary fluctuations along the way. While interest rates skyrocketed in general for a two-year period ending in spring 1980, there were at least three times in the last year of that cycle when they reversed themselves sharply for brief periods, a few weeks or less. These abrupt reversals sent the stock and bond markets gyrating wildly, providing the alert investor who follows these basic rules several opportunities to grab some quick profits.

Remember, all it takes to keep abreast of exactly what is going on, is a brief glance at the financial pages of your newspaper every few days or so. The *Wall Street Journal* and *Barron's* are, of course, the most complete financial newspapers in the country. It's worth making the investment to pick up *Barron's* once a week, on Saturdays when it comes out, and to buy the *Wall Street Journal* once or twice during the week.

A quick glance through both publications will tell you exactly where the DJIA is and what the money market funds are paying, just for starters. Various charts and graphs will also show you what the trends have been over the past few weeks or so, which gives you some idea of the direction things have been heading in.

Money supply figures, which are released every Friday afternoon, are now also an extremely important indicator of market activity. Week-to-week fluctuations are not nearly as important as the *cumulative* increase in monetary aggregates over the past quarter. If the nation's monetary base has grown at an annualized rate of 12 percent in the past quarter, for example, and this figure is higher than the preceding quarter, that is a pretty good sign that we are heading for double-digit inflation in fairly short order. Higher inflation ahead means higher interest rates a little later, so act accordingly. But if the rate of monetary expansion has been slowing down over the past few months, chances are that inflation might start to ease a bit in the months ahead, which will lead to lower interest rates and a healthier stock market.

Barron's publishes a list of money supply figures once a month on the inside last page. In April 1980 I noted that monetary growth for the past 12 months had been about 8.1 percent, which was down considerably from the prior year's growth. The annualized growth rate for the previous month was only 4.3 percent, which meant that the Fed had succeeded in slowing the growth rate in the nation's money supply, for the moment at least. If this continued (as it did for the next few months), it was a pretty good indication that the government had finally succeeded in breaking the back of the latest inflationary spiral.

The big question remaining was just how far down would the powers that be succeed in bringing inflation before they eased up and started pushing it back again? My guess was that, in order to cushion the effects of the impending recession, the authorities might ease up too soon and set us off on an even worse inflationary binge the next time around. My inclination was to move some money back into the stock market again, but for short-term trading profits only. With inflation probably easing and short-term rates continuing to fall, stocks should be getting ready for another quick spurt ahead.

FIXED INCOME

The bond market, as we have known it over the years, is now obsolete. In addition to bonds, the same statement holds true for preferred stocks, common utility stocks (strictly speaking utility stocks are not fixed-income securities, since they increase their dividends periodically, but I have included them here since people buy them for income the same way they buy bonds and preferreds, and utility stocks tend to fluctuate more like bonds than like other common stocks), and everything else that people have traditionally bought primarily for income and stability.

This does *not* mean that you can no longer buy these securities. It does mean that you should buy them only when the timing is right and should be prepared to trade them for profit when the market turns against you.

In the distant past of three or four years ago, bonds and utilities were considered suitable investments for retirees, fiduciary accounts, pension funds, superconservative trust accounts, and widows who depended on the income as their sole means of support. Now, because of the new rules we are forced to operate under, they have turned out to be among the most treacherous investments of all.

A man who worked hard all his life and managed to put together, say, $200,000 for his retirement could have bought a portfolio of bonds and utilities a few years back that would have provided him with an income of about $17,000 a year to live on. It seemed pretty reasonable at the time: nice safe investments throwing off about 8½ percent in interest and dividends. Two years later inflation in the United States started to push ahead into double digits again. No matter, thought this investor; it had happened before and it was only a matter of time before the government would get it back under control.

The value of the portfolio began to slip a bit to throw off higher yields for new buyers searching for better returns.* A portfolio once worth $200,000 was soon worth $190,000, then $185,000. At this point the retiree was beginning to get a little nervous; his principal was declining and the $17,000 income wasn't buying as much as it used to. Pretty soon the cycle had to end, he insisted. How long could this go on?

Just when it seemed that the worst had passed, that things could only improve from this point on, inflation zoomed ahead another couple of points. "This economy is out of control," cried our hypothetical retiree. "The 'experts' don't know what the hell they're doing anymore." Interest rates kept going up ferociously; in an effort to break the back of inflation. Utilities that yielded 8½ or 9 percent when the retiree bought them had fallen to a point where they yielded 14½ percent in early 1980.* Bonds that were bought for par with interest rates of 8 percent were now worth 60 cents on the dollar. The original $200,000 portfolio was now valued at *$120,000.* And the once attractive $17,000 income was now buying only half of what it bought four short years ago!

The man who thought he was semirich when he retired now felt like a denizen of Poverty Row. Chances are he will never be made whole again, and even if he does get back up to $200,000 in a year or so, his money will be worth less than $100,000 in terms of the value it had in the late 1970s. This person has been victimized by the new rules—more brutally, perhaps, than anyone else. Yet this is the fate that awaits anyone who decides to

---

*When interest rates go up, the prices of bonds and fixed-income securities go down to give higher returns to investors.

set up a fixed-income portfolio and simply hold on to it in the years ahead. The next bout of inflation could make the previous one look like a warm-up exercise. And even if this doesn't come to pass, it certainly pays all of us to be prepared for the worst.

As far as fixed-income securities are concerned, the best time to buy them is when interest rates appear to be *coming down*.

These securities fluctuate *counter* to interest rates; they move up in value when rates are falling and vice versa. If interest rates come down sharply you can expect a strong rally in bonds and other income-oriented securities.

Sometimes the bond and stock markets move together in the same direction, and sometimes they move in opposite directions. During the first few weeks of 1980, for example, while interest rates continued to soar, the bond market took a dreadful pounding while the stock market staged a strong rally for six weeks. The reason was that people expected rates to go even higher and were pulling money out of the bond market as fast as they could. Money moved into the stock market until such time as the yields on money market instruments soared into the teens. Then they sold stocks and bought short-term paper to take advantage of the safe high yields there. When these short-term rates started to fall in April 1980, this was a signal to take some money out of the money market and move it back into bonds and utilities, since they move up when interest rates fall. As rates continue to fall you can then expect to see some profit-taking in the bonds and utilities and this cash moving into stocks again, with the DJIA under 800 and so many good-quality stocks selling at bargain-basement prices.

Think of money as a fluid stream constantly moving to seek out the best possible return for itself. There is no mystery about it. The big trick is trying to stay ahead of the various markets as they keep changing before our eyes.

When buying bonds, stick to those maturing no more than *two* or *three years* out. They won't fluctuate as quickly as long-term bonds, but there will be enough movement in a volatile market to give you opportunity for a trade. And if you should happen to guess wrong and the market suddenly turns against you, you only have a couple of years to wait in order to get par value for the bonds. You don't want to be holding bonds that are showing a loss for 25 or 30 years just to get your money back, like the retiree we discussed a moment ago.

Also, buy bonds that are selling at a *discount* from par. You'll sacrifice some income in doing so, but the *built-in capital gain* over the next two or three years until the bonds mature will be taxed at a lower rate than ordinary income.

Since stocks have no maturity dates, you do not have to worry about this when buying preferreds and utility common shares. The utility market also staged a sharp recovery at the first sign of a downturn in short-term interest rates in April 1980. Some of them moved up 3 and 4 points in less than a month, enough to give you a chance for a quick trade, thereby freeing up cash for your next move into growth stocks.

GOLD AND SILVER

The best way to buy gold and silver is to own it outright, either by purchasing one-ounce gold coins and silver bars from a reputable bank or dealer, or by buying certificates that are fully backed by one or both metals. These types of products, such as Krugerrands and gold certificates, have been proliferating over the past couple of years as investors have grown more aware of precious metals as a hedge against inflation.

If inflation continues to plague us in the future as it did throughout the 1970s, you can expect to see both metals advance sharply in value from their present levels. (Other metals will also go up, but these two are the most accessible for investment purposes.) On the other hand, there has been more and more talk lately, both in Europe and the United States, about remonetizing gold to one degree or another. The Europeans are considering issuing some sort of joint currency partially backed by gold, and some leading Democrats and Republicans in this country have publicly discussed the possibility of doing the same with the dollar. This would tend to stabilize the price of gold (and other precious metals) at some agreed-upon level, probably in the neighborhood of $1,000 an ounce, and it would also have a dampening effect on inflation throughout the international arena.

My own guess is that this development, if it occurs at all, will not take place until the middle of the 1980s at the earliest. It will take at least that long to work out a system agreeable to all parties, and there is bound to be too much opposition from a broad range of interest groups for remonetization to take place smoothly or quickly. Also, the discipline it would impose on government would be too severe for politicians who have grown accustomed over the past few decades to spending tax dollars like so many drunken sailors. We might as well ask a happy alcoholic to voluntarily give up the bottle and take up drinking milk for a change.

Out-of-control inflation may one day force the authorities to impose some sort of restraint, possibly gold-related, on monetary growth, but for the next few years at least I expect to see gold and silver gyrating rather violently with inflationary cycles.

The best time to pick up some Krugerrands or silver bars for your portfolio is when inflation is in an *upswing*. When interest rates are mounting, drawing money from both the bond and stock markets, you should start to think about moving your cash into *precious metals* as well as money market instruments. In other words, when it is time to buy short-term paper, it is usually also time to pick up some gold. Actually, you will do better to buy your gold and silver in advance, at the first hint of rising inflation, since gold will start moving up before interest rates are high enough to make treasury bills an irresistible attraction.

In May 1980 gold was approximately $500 an ounce, and on any given day, it could fluctuate $20 or more. At the peak of that cycle, when it soared to $875 an ounce, the metal actually jumped $100 an ounce overnight at one point. Whenever inflation drops significantly I hesitate to buy either gold or silver, since they ordinarily drop to lower levels. But if the government eases up too quickly on monetary policy and settles for a high new bottom around 7 percent, I would then load up on gold coins and begin selling them off, one at a time in the same manner of stock shares, as gold advances to new highs. Also, as in the case with stocks, hold some coins in reserve so that you can participate if the metal does climb to the stratospheric heights some people are talking about—$2,000 an ounce and beyond.

Gold has been the most accurate barometer of inflation in the world throughout history. One way of looking at it is that gold hasn't really fluctuated at all for the most part; paper currencies have fluctuated, mostly downward, against it. In 1900 the average British worker earned half an ounce of gold a week. Today he still earns half an ounce of gold a week. The only difference is that the paper units he gets paid have multiplied considerably as the pound has drifted lower in value against that half ounce of gold.

The same is true of any other currency. If the dollar loses half its buying power over the next few years because of inflation, gold will probably be roughly double what it is today, or about $1,000 an ounce. Silver, too, has now joined gold as an inflationary hedge, although it is not nearly so accurate a barometer.

If the day does arrive when the authorities talk seriously about backing paper money with gold, it will then be time to sell your precious metals and put your cash in something else. Inflationary times will be over for a while.

One cautionary note: after you are finished paying a sales premium and taxes on your purchase of coins and bars, you will need a decent move, roughly 20 percent, just to break even. With gold at $500 an ounce it will cost you roughly $550 to buy a one-ounce coin after markup and sales tax. That means you need a move up to almost $600 to sell your coin for a small profit. You can narrow this spread somewhat by buying in volume, of course, but you need a lot of money for that. Still, with the volatile markets we have today, this may not seem like such a bad deal if inflation starts to get out of hand again.

I do *not* recommend the futures market as a means of speculating in gold. If your timing is off just a notch, you can get wiped out in a single trading session. When you own precious metals outright, however, you are in a position to bide your time and wait for the market to move in your favor.

Now let's take a look at some Automatic Trigger Signals, and then we will run through some scenarios to see how this program works in action.

4

Automatic Trigger Signals

Make a copy of this section and keep it in your wallet, pocketbook, or desk drawer for easy reference. These automatic trigger signals (ATS) will serve as a ready reminder of what you should be doing with your money after you have glanced through the financial pages of your newspaper.

DJIA 780–800

Time to buy stocks if yields on money market instruments are less than 12 percent. Check these yields before committing cash to the stock market.

DJIA under 780

This could be a negative sign that interest rates are going higher. If yields on money market funds have been rising during the past few weeks, do not commit money to the stock market yet.

Short-term rates 12 percent or more

Put your cash in a money market fund or treasury bills. If rates are rising, subscribe to three-month bills. If they are falling, subscribe to six-month bills. Buy bills in the Monday auction rather than on the open market, since you will get a better yield that way.

DJIA 850 and trending up

Start taking some quick profits with a small part of your stock holdings. Wait for the market to move above 900 or for one or more of your stocks to advance another few points.

DJIA 900 and trending up

Sell additional shares and move a little more heavily into a cash position. As you free up cash, put the proceeds into a money market fund.

DJIA 950 and trending up

Sell off more shares, so that you are holding roughly 20 percent of your original shares at this point. Get ready for total evacuation if the market breaks down below 900 again.

DJIA 1000 and trending up

Maintain 10 percent of your original position and take profits in the rest of your stocks. This way you will be able to participate if the market keeps advancing, but you are largely in a cash position now in the event of a sell-off.

DJIA 1050 and trending up

Whenever the DJIA is above 1050, turn to Part II of this book for additional signals.

DJIA 950 and falling

Maintain 5 percent of your original position, but be prepared to buy stocks back again if the market turns around and starts advancing. As you free up cash, continue to put the proceeds in a money market fund or into treasury bills.

DJIA 900 and falling

Move out of stocks entirely and into cash. If the market levels and moves back up over 900, buy a few shares back cautiously. Be prepared to abandon them if the market breaks down below 900 again.

Short-term rates starting to move above 10 percent

Start buying gold and/or silver with 5 to 10 percent of your money. At no time would I want to have more than 15 percent of my assets invested in gold or silver. Sell your bonds, utilities, and preferred stocks.

Short-term rates starting to move above 13 percent

Avoid the stock market like the plague. Put your money in a money market fund and in three-month treasury bills. Increase your position in gold and/or silver to 15 percent. Borrow money and invest it in treasury bills if you can afford the monthly carrying charges.

Short-term rates leveling above 15 percent

Start buying utilities and bonds maturing no more than three years out. Sell gold and silver and move more cash into the fixed-income market.

Short-term rates falling below 15 percent

Move more heavily into the fixed-income market. Lighten up on treasury bills and buy more bonds and utilities.

Short-term rates falling below 12 percent

Get ready to start moving money back into the stock market if the DJIA is under 800. Get out of treasury bills, keep some cash reserves in a money market fund, and cautiously start buying stocks. If inflation starts to fall, move more heavily into stocks. If it remains stubbornly high, keep most of your money in a money market fund.

Inflation starts to fall

Start buying stocks if the DJIA is under 800. Also buy some bonds with short maturities and some utilities.

Inflation starts to rise

Get out of the stock and bond market. Put cash in a money market fund. Start buying gold and silver.

Monetary growth is slowing down

Start buying stocks if the DJIA is under 800. Buy utilities and bonds with short maturities.

Monetary growth is speeding up

Start buying gold and silver. Move money into money market instruments. Get out of stocks and bonds. Start borrowing money if you can afford the payments.

A conservative has just been elected president

Buy stocks for quick trading profits, then be prepared to sell them as soon as he assumes office. Tight-money policies will hurt the stock market during his first year or so in office.

A liberal has just been elected president

Get out of the stock market immediately. Be prepared to buy stocks after he has been in office a few months, since loose money will fuel the economy in the beginning. Keep your eye on the inflation figures, however, and get ready to jump when they turn upward.

War is threatened overseas

A minor skirmish will not hurt the stock market and may, in fact, be good for certain aspects of it, such as defense and aerospace stocks. A large war, however, involving American forces is, contrary to popular opinion, a strong negative for the market. Buy gold, silver, and other doomsday hedges if the news is exceedingly bad.

General Comments

The stock market can usually be expected to hit bottom about two or three months into a recession; the tricky part is trying to figure out exactly when a recession has begun.

The experts started predicting a recession late in 1978, agreeing almost unanimously that it would occur sometime during the first half of 1979. By April 1979 it was apparent to everyone who had taken Economics 101 that the American economy was, if anything, heating up even more, instead of cooling off the way it was supposed to. Inflation was moving up alarmingly and rising interest rates failed to slow it in the least.

As 1979 ground to a close without any hint of a recession on the horizon, the experts ate a little crow and predicted once again that the elusive recession would hit us sometime early in 1980. By the end of the first quarter of 1980, the official figures seemed to confirm the fact that a recession had already taken hold or was soon about to. Newspapers were filled with stories of layoffs, particularly in the automobile industry, and slowdowns already taking place throughout the economy. At this time it was a fairly safe bet that a recession had begun.

This being the case, the time for acquiring stocks again was near at hand. This leads us to another *automatic trigger signal* that is not as clearly defined as those I listed above.

When the worst economic news starts making the front pages of the newspapers, it is time to think about buying stocks.

In other words, when most people have already panicked out of the market and the overall outlook is most gloomy— that is usually the best time to get back in. Conversely, when the general mood is most euphoric and people seem to feel that everything is moving along hummingly, that is the time to think about taking your profits and holing up for a while. This little bit of general Contrarian theory works like a charm. Do the *opposite* of what everyone else is doing, and you'll make out just fine.

The final comment I want to make before moving on to the next section is to caution you to *always be prepared for surprises*. No cycle runs smoothly. During every upswing in stock prices, every run-up in inflation and interest rates, and every decline, there are always ups and downs along the way. The market may go up for a bit, turn south again and hit a false bottom, then start to rally briefly, only to turn back down below its previous false bottom. This pattern holds true on both sides of a cycle, upside and downside. There are bear traps and bull traps all over the place as the various markets whipsaw up and down.

Don't let yourself get whipsawed!

Keep your eye on the general trend and expect the unexpected along the way. If you do a little homework, an hour or so a week, keep your eye on the DJIA, on the money supply figures, on short-term yields, on the trend in inflation, you'll do just fine.

We'll take a look now at how this plan works in action.

5

The Plan in Action

You are a middle-class investor, not rich but not poor, who had $50,000 in liquid assets back in 1978. With this money you decided to keep $10,000 in cash in a money market fund and invest the other $40,000 in several of the stocks I recommended.

After the October sell-off in 1978, you noticed that the DJIA had leveled a little below 800, yields on short-term paper were under 10 percent, and inflation was still below 10 percent but starting to inch up. In December of 1978 you loaded up on stocks after checking the list of Automatic Trigger Signals—ATS—in the preceding section. Inflation was bothering you, but interest rates had not started to advance significantly, so you decided to hold off on gold or silver investments until the trends were more clearly defined.

Your timing was perfect and the market got off to a rollicking start shortly after you bought your stocks. The market kept climbing as the year got underway, not a blockbuster rally, but a good steady advance. Meanwhile the inflation figures were getting worse. The anticipated recession had failed to materialize, and the current inflation rate was somewhere around 13 percent and rising. Interest rates started to climb a bit and you decided to take some profits in your stocks, and move some cash into a few Krugerrands.

The economy continued to gallop along at a fairly brisk pace and there was no sign of a recession in sight. The money supply figures were also growing at a double-digit rate, despite the government's claim it was following a tight-money policy. Inflation could only move higher and interest rates were sure to follow. You sold some more stock and put some cash into the money market fund, and bought another couple of Krugerrands. Your position now looked like this:

> $30,000 in the stock market
> $20,600 in a money market fund
> $5,000 in gold

You've made a $5,000 profit on your stocks so far and another $600 interest in the money market fund.

In June 1979 Carter appointed Paul Volcker chairman of the Federal Reserve. His first act on the job was to tighten the screws on interest rates. Inflation was still climbing and yields on short-term paper were pushing through 10 percent. You decided to take additional profits on your stocks with the DJIA up near 900. Your portfolio was now diversified in the following manner:

> $20,000 in the stock market
> $32,850 in a money market fund
> $5,000 in gold

Your equity was now up to $57,850 due to profits in the stock market and interest in the money market fund. Inflation remained persistently high, gold was starting to jump ahead faster than it had ever moved before, the DJIA was above 900, and short-term interest rates had just moved into the low teens. You consulted the ATS and made your decision. In September 1979 you decided to abandon the market entirely. Now you had:

> $0 in the stock market
> $56,050 in a money market fund
> $10,000 in gold, which had doubled

Your equity was $66,050 and you started a year earlier with $50,000, for a 32 percent return. Gold kept on rolling ahead to $800 an ounce and you decided to sell half your coins and hold the others in reserve. The market crash landed just under 800 on the Dow by December. The experts said a recession had not yet begun. The yield on the money market fund was 11½ percent. You consulted the ATS and here's what you saw:

> *DJIA:* 800
> *Short-term rates:* 11½ percent
> *Inflation:* 15 percent
> *Money supply growth:* stable but still high

What do you do?

According to the DJIA indicator, the market was a buy. Short-term interest rates seemed to be approaching a borderline situation. According to the inflation indicator, gold still looked good but might be nearing a top if inflation leveled off. According to money supply figures, gold also looked like it might be nearing a top. So you decided to

1. Buy some stocks, but not heavily since those short-term interest rates will hurt the market if they go any higher;

2. Keep a substantial amount of cash in the money market fund;

3. Sell off half your gold, which by now had tripled.

Your portfolio now looked like this:

> $10,000 in the stock market
> $55,000 in a money market fund
> $7,500 in gold

Beginning in the early days of January 1980, the market started to roll. Volume was increasing every day as the market advanced steadily toward the 900 level. Gold was also leaping as it never had before, and the value of your coins was up to $12,000. But then came another ATS. In the effort to curb inflation, which was now pushing 18 percent on an annualized basis, the Fed was jacking up interest rates a percentage point at a time. The prime was now at 18 percent and short-term rates were up to 14 percent in the money market fund. In the middle of February, following a spectacular month-and-a-half-long rally, the DJIA stood at 905.

The ATS were as follows:

> *DJIA:* 905
> *Short-term rates:* 14 percent
> *Monetary growth:* still increasing, despite higher interest
> rates
> No sign of a recession
> *Inflation:* not yet under control

The ATS told you to sell your stocks and move this cash back into the money market. You also sold half your gold, which had quadrupled over the past six months, and your position now looked like this:

> $0 in the stock market
> $73,600 in a money market fund
> $5,000 in gold

Since the yields on treasury bills had just reached 15 percent (they would eventually peak at 16½ percent for three-month bills) you decided to put $40,000 into three-month bills and leave the balance of the cash in the money market fund.

Again the ATS worked like a charm. No sooner did you sell your stocks when the stock market came unglued. Beginning in the middle of February, a sell-off took place that made the January rally look puny by comparison. Never before in history did the stock market have to compete with treasury bills, and other virtually risk-free short-term paper, yielding over 15 percent. Money flew out of the stock market and into the money markets faster than the speed of light. The first ten days of the collapse were positively breathtaking, with the market giving back the entire gain it had made over the past six weeks. In ten mad, stupefying days, the stock market crashed over 100 points, dropping from a peak of 905 to just below 800.

And still the selling would not let up. When it looked as though all panic selling was finally over, forced margin selling knocked the market down another 20 points. The prime rate was pushed up to an all-time high of 20 percent, treasury bills were up to 16½ percent for three-month paper, and money market funds were yielding 18 percent. The signals looked like this:

> DJIA: 780 and falling
> Short-term rates: in the high teens
> Monetary growth: high but leveling
> Inflation: 18 percent and leveling

The ATS told you to keep your cash in the money market with short-term rates as high as this. Also, the fact that the DJIA was about to break down below 780 was another negative indicator for the stock market. You decided to stay put.

The selling in the stock market continued for week after week at a brutalizing pace. Finally, after nearly two and a half months of it, we seemed to be making a turn. The DJIA had sunk as low as 735, rallied briefly to 790, pulled back again to 770, and hovered in this area on low volume and quiet trading. The prime rate was lowered at a few major banks to 19½ percent, then to 19 percent and 18½ percent a week or so later. The latest figures seemed to indicate that a recession had already begun. Inflation appeared to be topping out an an annualized 18 percent. And the growth in monetary aggregates had slowed considerably over the previous three months. The ATS now read as follows:

DJIA: 790
Short-term rates: 12 percent and falling
Inflation: apparently under control
Monetary growth: declining
A recession apparently already begun

The ATS were telling you to:
1. Start buying stocks again;
2. Start buying short-term bonds and utilities;
3. Either sell your gold or hold it as a hedge in case you read the signals wrong.

In late April 1980, after avoiding the stock market for a solid ten weeks as though it were contaminated, you decided to get back in again. You also decided to buy some bonds and utilities as well, but you also decided to hang on to your gold, since inflation was still inordinately high and the Fed might have been dropping interest rates prematurely in the hopes of avoiding a severe recession with an election approaching in six months. Your portfolio now looked like this:

> $30,000 in the stock market
> $40,000 in treasury bills (maturing in late May)
> $6,200 in a money market fund
> $3,000 in gold, which fell to $500 an ounce

Our total equity of over $79,000 represents nearly a 60 percent return in about a year and a half. All this was accomplished, of course, with the benefit of 20-20 hindsight and the resulting simplification of our ATS, which are never as clearly defined in the present as they are in retrospect. As I mentioned earlier, no cycle in any market is ever smooth; there are always pullbacks on the upside and false rallies on the downside, and it is easy to get whipsawed if you are not careful.

The main point, however, is that the signals will work if they are followed unemotionally. *Money always seeks out the best possible return for itself.* This is the one irrevocable, irrefutable law of the marketplace. There is no emotion or morality involved. When the stock market is low, people will buy stocks if they cannot get better returns elsewhere. When those returns are available in the money market, which involves little if any risk, money will flow in that direction. When people are concerned about inflation or international catastrophe, they will put their money in gold and other doomsday hedges.

The ATS I have presented here are based on the new rules that have been imposed on us during the South Americanization of our economy. They are based on economic realities as they have evolved in rapid order during the past couple of years. My own opinion right now is that the federal government will settle for a relatively high bottom on the next downward cycle in inflation in order to soften the effect of what could turn out to be a rather nasty recession. If this is true, the next upswing in inflation could be even worse than the last, leading to another round of record-high interest rates.

If I am wrong, my ATS will tell me so and I will act accordingly. That's the beauty of these signals. You don't have to be a genius or a prophet to make money with your investments. All you have to do is look at the ATS and do what they tell you to do. A perusal of your newspaper once or twice a week is all the time it will take you to make your investment decisions.

Next we'll take a look at some relatively easy ways to shelter all those short-term profits we're going to be making.

6

How to Shelter Your Income and Profits

There is a good deal of confusion regarding the subject of tax shelters. This is unfortunate, because the basic concept is a simple one to grasp. Much of this confusion has to be laid at the doorstep of lawyers and accountants, who have deliberately complicated the ground rules so that the average investor must turn to them to unravel the mystery.

Tax-related investments fall into three broad categories: tax-free, tax-*deferred,* and tax-*sheltered.*

Tax-free income is achieved by investing in municipal bonds, the interest from which is not subject to federal and, sometimes, state and local taxes. The interest from treasury bills, notes, and bonds, and from several additional types of government bonds is not subject to state and local taxes.

Tax-deferred income is income that is not subject *immediately* to *any* tax. Ordinarily you will receive income from an investment for a period of time, and only upon termination of the investment do you have to pay income tax or, in some cases, long-term capital gains tax on the income you have received over the years. Annuities, dividends from certain utility stocks, and limited partnerships in real estate and other deals are the most popular means of getting tax-deferred income.

Both tax-free and tax-deferred investments are made with *after-*tax dollars. Once you have paid your taxes, and if you are fortunate enough to have some legal tender left to invest, you can then invest these dollars in the first two categories.

The third category, the one we are primarily concerned with here, is tax-*sheltered* investments. A tax shelter is anything you can do with *pre*-tax dollars. It is anything that allows you to put money aside and then deduct this money from your income *be-fore* you pay your taxes. Some tax shelters permit you to take a portion of these dollars off your gross income, some the full amount, and a dwindling few permit you to take a multiple of the investment off your gross income. It is this great phenomenon called tax shelters that makes it possible for some very rich people, including some top politicians who are responsible for the tax laws in the first place, to get away with paying little or no taxes at all.

Let's take a look at some of the best, and most obvious, shelters available to the average individual.

YOUR HOUSE

By far the single best tax shelter you have, and probably ever will have, is your house. It is the best shelter imaginable because (1) it allows you to deduct dollars from your pre-tax income; (2) it is a margin investment with no downside risk—that is, even under the worst of circumstances you cannot be subject to a margin call; (3) it has proven to be the most reliable means of building equity for the future; and (4) if you sell it properly you can avoid paying capital gains tax on it.

Since your house (or condominium or cooperative apartment) is such a spectacular tax shelter, the most amazing thing of all is that so many people fail to utilize it to the fullest. Even today, after all that has been said about inflation and taxes, many investors with good sustainable income are still afraid to borrow on their homes to the extent they should. With inflation as high as it is and likely to remain at least annoyingly high in the foreseeable future, with middle-income wage earners being forced into higher tax brackets that are not indexed for inflation, it is *economic suicide* not to mortgage the hell out of your home as your equity increases.

The major reason why people don't refinance their homes every few years is a fear that they won't be able to keep up with higher mortgage payments. Yet assuming that you maintain your income and reinvest the borrowed dollars instead of blowing them on a trip around the world, the numbers *have* to work in your favor.

Anyone making more than $45,000 a year today is in a 50 percent tax bracket. With more wives working now than ever before, the two-income, high-income family is more the rule than the exception. Let's assume this couple decided to take out a second mortgage on their home back in February 1980, when mortgage rates were at their highest. They borrowed $10,000 at 16 percent interest, payable over 15 years. Their monthly payments come to $146 a month, of which approximately $137 is interest and, there-fore, deductible from their gross income. At the time they bor-rowed this money, tax-free bonds were yielding better than 10 percent (as it turned out, they were also a good buy, since it was the top of the interest-rate cycle. See Chapter Four.) By investing this $10,000 in tax-free bonds, our couple was able to generate an income of $1,000 a year, or $83 a month, free and clear of taxes.

It is true that there is a $63-a-month shortfall between in-creased income and new expenditures, but this is only in pre-tax dollars. When they deduct the $137 a month in interest payments from their gross income, they will actually be paying only $77 a month to the bank in *hard, after-tax* dollars. They are actually making a few dollars a month on the deal, and they have created an extra $10,000 in cash money for themselves, which is a nice cushion to be sitting on. This couple has, in effect, taken equity out of their home and put it into a *liquid* investment. As their incomes go up over the years, they will be able to make the extra payment more easily and free up that $10,000 for other purposes if they want to.

This is a nice, cautious, conservative approach to the situation. A more aggressive couple might decide to take the $10,000 and invest it in the fashion I outlined in Chapter Three. This is cer-tainly the approach I would take myself, since I am not a fan of tax-free bonds except for trading purposes. The above exercise, however, demonstrates that you really do make money by bor-rowing on your house. You've got liquid cash money in hand and a true tax shelter for your income and profits.

A SECOND HOME

If you can afford it, a second house is an even *better* shelter than the one you live in, providing you rent it out. If you own a second home and use it for enjoyment on weekends, you can deduct the interest payments and taxes from your income, the same as with your main house, but you are not entitled to the extra shelter benefits.

The best way to utilize your second home as a tax shelter is not to use it personally for more than 14 days a year. You can vacation in it yourself for two weeks a year, but no more, and still get full write-off on it.

If possible, buy a new second home, since you will then be able to depreciate it more advantageously than a used home. A new second home can be depreciated at 8 percent a year, while a used second home can only be depreciated at a 5 percent annual rate.

It works like this. You are in the 50 percent tax bracket and you decide to buy a new second home for $50,000. You rent it out full time except for two weeks a year, when you use it for your own vacation. The tax laws allow you to take $4,000 a year (or 8 percent of $50,000), in addition to interest payments on the mortgage and property taxes, right off your income. The depreciation alone saves you $2,000 a year in taxes, since you would have paid this much to Uncle Sam on the $4,000 had you not been able to take it off your income. A used second home, also used as an investment in the above way, would give you a $2,500 annual write-off (5 percent of the purchase price).

Besides writing off depreciation, taxes, and interest payments on your second home, the tax laws also permit you to deduct:

1. Maintenance costs, including money you pay your children to work on the house. By doing this you are, in effect, shifting income from your high bracket to your children, who are presumably in a lower bracket.

2. Furniture and other furnishings for the second home can be depreciated, and 10 percent of the purchase price can be taken as a tax *credit*, which is far superior to a simple deduction from income. For example, if it costs you $2,000 to furnish your second home, you can reduce your actual tax payments by $200.

3. Traveling back and forth between your first and second homes is another deductible expense.

If you are going to buy a second home as a tax shelter, you would be well advised to find a tax man who is thoroughly familiar with the laws in this area to make sure you get full advantage of all the write-offs you are entitled to. A second home utilized in this fashion is really a business, and it is treated as such by the law.

YOUR CREDIT CARDS

Curse them though we may, credit cards are another legitimate tax shelter, as well as one of the great bargains of modern civilization. If they weren't, the banks, department stores, oil companies, and other issuers of credit wouldn't have started screaming back in the spring of 1980 that they were being ripped off by the public. They raised hell in Washington, D.C., via their assorted lobbyists, twisting arms and knocking heads in order to get the government to limit the use of credit throughout the country. The Carter administration finally complied, tightening the screws on overdraft privileges in checking accounts, lines of credit on various cards, and general bank loans for anything except home-related expenses. For a while there it seemed you had to be a failing corporation or a billionaire silver trader to get a loan anywhere.

The sweet, beautiful irony of the situation was the fact that it was the federal government, the banks, and the various issuers of credit who made it so enticing for people to borrow money in the first place. Borrowing was never a bargain for anyone before the age of inflation, and we can thank government for presenting us with record-high inflation during the past decade. And it was the banks and department stores who kept mailing out all those plastic cards, begging the public to use them, back when it was profitable for them to do so. The public was seduced over a period of two decades to string itself out on credit. Most people went along reluctantly. It cut against the grain of our entire ethic; it was contrary to everything we had been taught in Sunday school: "Never a borrower or a lender be. A penny saved is a penny earned. Pay off your debts promptly." No, it was not the general public that ushered in the age of plastic money.

For a long time there the lenders had a pretty good deal going for themselves. With inflation ranging between 4 and 7 percent, they were charging 12 to 18 percent for money. The loan sharks never had it so good, since they didn't have the law on their side. Then, gradually, over a period of a few years, the worm began to turn. Inflation ran up into the high teens, the prime rate soared to 20 percent, and lenders were paying more for money than the people they were lending to. Suddenly they began to panic. *The system wasn't supposed to work this way!*

If you had run your credit cards up to the limit by February 1980 you were sitting in the catbird seat. You owed *all that money,* and the banks and department stores and the oil companies could *not* demand it back from you, not all at once anyway. If you had not used your cards—if you had, let's say, a $2,000 limit on your Visa card and you hadn't gotten around to using it yet—you were suddenly cut back to a $100 limit or maybe even zero. But assuming that you were in hock up to your eyeballs, the thing to do at this juncture was to pay them off *slowly,* to drag it out as long as you could. You were holding all the cards now. You had used all their money over the years, at what turned out to be bargain rates, and now there was a recession coming on and the creditors were getting nervous. People were losing jobs and the banks and creditors were worried about their ability to pay their debts. They *had* to be nice to you as long as you sent in the minimum amount each month.

Yes, the best course of action with high inflation here, and likely to remain with us for quite a spell, is to run your card up to the limit, send in the minimum monthly amount, and immediately charge it back on the card again. The creditors *can't* reduce your limit if you don't give them any room. As long as you keep your debt up close to the limit, there's not much the banks can do about it. Later on, if—miracle of miracles—the authorities succeed in bringing down inflation to 4 or 5 percent, and *keeping* it there for a few years or so, you then have the option of reducing your debt load. Right now, however, you are holding all the aces if you are in debt. And that 18, 20, or even 24 percent you may be paying for money is really costing you only half that rate after taxes. The interest comes right off the top, and that's what sheltering your income and profits is all about.

KEOGH ACCOUNTS

If you are self-employed, or if you have free-lance income outside of your salaried employment, you can shelter your income and profits in a Keogh account.

This type of a shelter allows you to put aside up to 15 percent of your free-lance income in a special retirement account. You can open a Keogh account with a bank in a savings plan offering a fixed income rate; you can do it through a mutual fund; or you can have a self-directed account with a brokerage firm, where you pick and choose your own investments with certain limited restrictions. The interest and dividends that accrue in a Keogh account are not taxed until they are withdrawn. The idea is that you will probably be in a lower tax bracket when you retire, and a Keogh account allows you to shelter income and investment profits until later on in life.

For example, if you are self-employed and make $50,000 a year which puts you in a 50 percent bracket, you can choose to put away as much as 15 percent, or $7,500 a year, in a Keogh account and save $3,750 in taxes that you would have owed on the $7,500 had you not sheltered it. Seven thousand five hundred dollars is the maximum amount you are allowed to shelter each year in Keogh. In addition to the initial investment, the dividends and interest accruing in the account are not taxed until they are withdrawn.

At present, this money must remain in your Keogh account until you are 59½ years of age, and it must be withdrawn by the time you are 70½ years old. The only way you can withdraw this money before 59½ without paying a substantial penalty is if you become disabled.

Once you reach the age of 59½ you can then elect to take your money out in several ways. You can withdraw it in a lump sum, in regular installments over a fixed period of time, or a combination of ways that might best be discussed with your tax adviser. A salaried employee could qualify for both an IRA account, which we will discuss shortly, and a Keogh account if he has free-lance income on the side.

If you own your own business and employ others, you *must* set up Keogh plans for those who have worked for you for at least three years and who work a minimum of 1,000 hours a year. The percentage of income you contribute for your employees must equal the same percentage you shelter for yourself. Using the example we used a moment ago, let's suppose you earn $50,000 a year as a self-employed consultant and you shelter 15 percent of your income each year in a Keogh account. You also employ a full-time secretary who has worked for you for at least three years. You are required to put aside 15 percent of her income each year in a separate retirement fund for her, and this shelter must be financed by you. You are not obligated to do this if she has worked less than three years for you.

IRA ACCOUNTS

The concept of an Individual Retirement Account is essentially the same as Keogh, the main distinction being that this is a shelter for salaried employees who are *not* covered by a pension or retirement plan at work.

If you fall in this category you can shelter up to 15 percent of your annual income in an IRA account, with the current maximum set at $1,500 a year. A working couple, neither of whom is covered by a pension plan at work, can shelter $1,500 apiece in separate IRA accounts for a maximum combined tax shelter of $3,000 a year. If your spouse does *not* work, you can shelter an additional $250 a year in a spousal IRA plan, for total shelter amounting to $1,750.

If you are covered at present by a retirement plan at work and decide to move to another firm that does not have a pension setup, you are permitted to roll the money over into an IRA account, providing you do so within 60 days. In other words, assuming that you are vested in the retirement plan, you can take whatever money has accrued and put the entire amount into your own IRA account. The government has been talking about raising the maximum amount you can contribute annually into an IRA account, but so far it still stands at $1,500.

LIMITED PARTNERSHIPS

Various types of tax shelter programs exist that allow you deduct money right off the top of your income. Some of these offer the investor good prospect of financial gain over the years, and others do not.

The basic structure of most tax shelters is a limited partnership. A limited partnership offers you the opportunity to invest money in a business venture, deduct the investment, a portion of the investment, or a multiple of it from your income, and participate as a shareholder in the business. Your liability is limited to the amount of your investment, which means that you could conceivably lose your entire investment but are not liable for any additional losses suffered by the business. The primary role of limited partners is to provide the start-up money required for a venture. In return you are legally entitled to various tax benefits above and beyond the deduction of your investment from your income.

The management and operation of the business is entrusted to the general partner, who may or may not have his own money at risk. The primary goal of someone who buys into a tax shelter is the tax write-off that is permitted by law, but in most cases there is also the hope that the business venture will thrive and prosper, so that the profits and capital gains are passed along to the limited partners. The cash flow from successful tax shelters is also sheltered with substantial tax benefits.

Shelters come with varying degrees of risk attached. Generally speaking, the greater the amount of money you are allowed to deduct from your income, the greater the risk you will be assuming. The most popular forms of tax shelters today are oil and gas drilling ventures, real estate partnerships, and, for larger investors, equipment leasing, barge deals, boxcar partnerships, and other exotic variations with rather complicated legal ramifications.

The average individual, however, will be most concerned about oil and gas and real estate deals. The more conservative real estate programs are privately financed and usually involve prime residential or commercial property, such as garden apartment complexes and shopping centers. They ordinarily allow the limited partners to deduct the amount of the investment from their incomes, but no more than this amount. These are called "one-on-one deals," referring to the fact that a $10,000 investment, for example, permits you to deduct $10,000 from the top of your income. These programs offer the limited partner good economic investment as well. Usually there will be a return on the investment from rents, which is passed along to the limited partner, and then a capital gain several years later when the properties are sold and the profit on the sale divided among the partners. These are good, clean programs, sold to the public by major brokerage firms, offering moderate tax shelter and profit potential.

Subsidized real estate programs, on the other hand, offer the limited partners *multiple* write-offs on their investment, and little else. These are primarily for people with huge incomes, well above $100,000 a year, who are looking for a way to invest, say, $40,000 and deduct *three* and *four* times this amount from their income. A three-to-one write-off refers to the fact that an investor can put up, for example, $40,000 and take $120,000 off the top of his income. These deals are usually publicly funded housing projects for senior or low-income citizens. Since these are not ordinarily profit-making ventures, the huge write-off is the main attraction for investors.

Oil and gas ventures can also be high-risk or low-risk, depending on the needs and the temperament of the individual investor. Low-risk shelters are primarily "developmental"; that is, they are partnerships formed to drill for oil and gas in areas where there are known reserves—the money is put up to develop wells that are already producing. The allowable tax write-off here is smaller than it is for "exploratory" shelters, where the limited partners are investing money to explore for oil and gas in areas where it has not yet been found. Some shelter programs are called "combinations," referring to the fact that part of the wells are exploratory and the rest of the wells in the program are developmental. All these programs permit you to shelter all or a portion of your investment from your income, and they offer the prospect of cash flow to the limited partners if and when the wells produce.

Tax shelter programs of various kinds are sold to the investing public by major brokerage firms, and some are marketed by the general partners themselves through accountants and tax attorneys who, in turn, recommend them to their individual clients.

MISCELLANEOUS

Custodial Accounts. If you have children under 18 years of age, you might consider putting part of your assets in their names in a custodial account. Simply call up your broker and tell him or her that you want to open up a custodial account for your offspring.

The mechanics are simple. The account will read, "John Doe, Custodian for John Doe, Jr., under the Uniform Gift to Minors Act [under the state you live in]." Remember, if you decide to go this route, you are giving a gift to the child; his or her social security number is on the account, not yours, and when the child reaches majority age, 18 or 21 depending on the state, the assets in the account legally belong to the child. The benefit to the parent rests in the fact that all dividends and interest are taxed at the child's bracket, which in most cases will be nonexistent. To achieve this benefit, however, you have to be willing to give up the money in the first place, since the gift is irrevocable.

Clifford Trusts (Reversionary Trusts). If you prefer not to make an outright gift to your children, but would like to reap some tax benefits anyway, you might consider a Clifford or reversionary trust. This must be set up with the assistance of a lawyer and an accountant. In this case you are making a *temporary* gift to your offspring, and the assets will revert to you after a minimum period of time, usually ten years and one day. The income from your investments will, once again, be taxed at the child's bracket level, but in most cases the capital gains taxes will have to be paid by the parents. In some instances it may be possible to avoid this capital gains treatment, but this can be accomplished only with the help of a very sharp tax lawyer or accountant. The law is very finicky on this item, and the loopholes are tiny and hard to squiggle through.

There is also an estate tax consideration in both custodial accounts and Clifford trusts that you should be aware of. When you make a gift to a minor under the current law, you are permitted to give $3,000 a year per parent, for a total of $6,000 if the gift is made jointly, without suffering any tax liability whatsoever. If you exceed this annual amount, the excess must be added to the value of the donor's estate upon death, which will increase the estate taxes. This is significant, of course, only in the event of a very large estate. In the case of a Clifford trust, the parents are allowed to give as much as $13,586 without paying gift taxes on it.

Capital Losses. If you must take a loss on a stock or a bond (or any other investment for that matter), make sure your loss is short-term—which presently is a year or less. With a short-term loss, you can deduct the entire loss from your income in the year it occurs, up to a maximum of $3,000 a year. A loss in excess of this figure can be carried forward into the next year. Long-term losses can only be deducted at a rate of 50 cents on the dollar, which means a $1,000 loss will give you a $500 tax write-off.

Ideally, your gains should be long-term for the best possible tax treatment, since long-term gains are taxed at a maximum rate of 28 percent, while short-term gains are treated as ordinary income. As I said earlier, however, I prefer to take my gains as they occur and worry about sheltering them later. I'd rather take a short-term gain than watch it become a long-term loss.

Short Against the Box. If you do have a capital gain and want to defer the tax liability into the next year instead of the present one, tell your broker to sell your stock "short against the box." This means that your broker will lend you the stock you are selling and deliver it to the buyer. When the new year begins, you then cover your short position, that is, pay back your broker for the stock you borrowed by giving him your own stock, and the tax consequence will fall into the new year. People who expect their incomes to be lower the next year, who already have enough capital gains to worry about in the present year, or who simply want more time to think about sheltering their gains utilize this technique.

Return of Capital. When the automatic trigger signals tell you to buy fixed-income securities, consider buying tax-free bonds and utilities that pay tax-deferred dividends instead of fully taxable securities. Tax-free bonds are free of all federal taxes, and if you buy bonds issued within the state you live in they are free of state and local taxes as well. As far as utilities are concerned, ask your broker for a list of utilities paying tax-deferred dividends. Long Island Lighting, San Diego Gas & Electric, Ohio Edison, Portland General, and American Electric Power are just a few that come to mind.

Some of these are completely tax-deferred, some partially. All or part of the dividends are treated as a return of capital. You pay no taxes on the tax-deferred portion until you elect to sell the stock. When you do, you are supposed to deduct the untaxed dividends from your cost, subtract the reduced cost from your selling price, and pay a capital gains tax on the difference. This is significant if you hold these stocks for longer than a year, since you are then converting ordinary income into long-term capital gains.

Deductions. Last but not least, become as thoroughly knowledgeable about the latest tax laws as you possibly can. While we hire accountants and lawyers to advise us on how to best reduce our tax exposure, it doesn't hurt to be as much on top of the situation as time allows. Accountants often overlook deductible items, particularly for their smaller clients, and you should therefore be thinking about taxes all year long, not just at the end of the year. Every large brokerage firm publishes a booklet condensing the tax code into a compact, easy-to-read, easy-to-follow list of essential items. Don't be afraid to call your broker and ask for it. This is one of the services you are paying him all those commissions for.

Remember, while you are consulting the ATS and making your investment decisions accordingly, think taxes! think taxes! think taxes!

7

The Automatic Trigger Signals Pass the Test

Those who are already following the ATS have discovered that they worked like a charm. In Chapter Five, with interest rates falling, inflation apparently leveling, monetary growth declining, and a recession having recently begun, I made the following statement:

> The ATS were telling you to:
> 1. Start buying stocks again;
> 2. Start buying short-term bonds and utilities;
> 3. Either sell your gold or hold it as a hedge in case you read the signals wrong.
>
> In late April 1980, after avoiding the stock market for a solid ten weeks as though it were contaminated, you decided to get back in again.

By October 1980 the stock market had been rallying solidly for the previous five months and the DJIA has just shot past the 970 mark. Interest rates had fallen to the point where treasury bills yielded less than 8 percent and money market funds yielded about 9 percent. Although interest rates started to move up again in late summer, and could be a threat if they continued higher, the general trend was still downward. Monetary growth had begun to expand after a period of contraction, and inflation remained stubbornly high. Following my own advice, I started accumulating stocks heavily in late April in my own account and in the accounts of people whose money I manage. These are the stocks I bought, with their purchase prices and the prices they had reached by October 1980:

Company	Purchase price	Current price
RCA	20¾	32
Pittston	18⅞	28
Howard Johnson	16⅜	Taken over at $28 a share
Allis Chalmers	23⅜	31
Savin	13½	15¾
Virginia Electric	11⅝	12⅛
Lear Siegler	19½	28
G. C. Murphy	14⅛	16½
Portland General	14⅝	14⅞
Brunswick	11⅝	15
Scott Paper	16⅝	19½
Oklahoma Gas & Electric	14	15
Imperial Oil	36⅛	42⅛
Ralston Purina	10¼	13¼
Hoover	13⅝	18
Northeast Utilities	9¼	9⅝
Clorox	8⅞	11⅞
American Family	8	8⅞
Westinghouse	22¾	28
Heublein	25¼	34½
Merrill Lynch	21¼	33
El Paso Co.	16⅞	26
Bally	24½	28⅝

As you can see, there was not a loss in 23 stock selections, and some of them were up more than 10 points. In addition, I chose high-quality, defensive stocks, that is, those paying well-covered dividends yielding a minimum of 6 percent and some as high as 12½ percent, and selling for anywhere from 3 to 6 times earnings. In November 1980, the ATS signals were as follows:

> *DJIA:* 990 and rising
> *Short-term rates:* above 10 percent and leveling
> *Inflation:* falling slowly
> *Monetary growth:* expanding
> A recession approximately 10 months old (the government, in its infinite wisdom, put the official beginning of the recession at January 1980)

Referring to Chapter Four's Automatic Trigger Signals we see at a glance that the signals are telling us to:

1. Sell off shares of stock and move some of the cash into a money market fund;

2. Keep buying utilities and other fixed-income securities with part of the proceeds from the stock sales;

3. Hold some shares in reserve just in case the market keeps on rallying beyond the 1000 level on the DJIA;

4. Be ready to abandon stocks altogether if the DJIA pulls back below 900;

5. If we already own gold, maintain the present position. Make new purchases of precious metals if interest rates and inflation continue moving back up again;

6. Refer to Part II if the DJIA rises above 1050.

A few years ago it would normally have taken the economy a year or longer to pass from the circumstances we had in April 1980 to those that were prevalent in November 1980. But because of the South Americanization of the United States and the resulting violence it has produced in our market cycles, these drastic swings are taking place within weeks and months now, instead of months and years.

For this reason it is more important than ever before to pay close attention to the ATS and consult them at least once a week, if not more frequently. In October 1980, following my own advice, I took some profits in many of the stocks I had bought, and was prepared to get out of the market entirely once the signals told me to. Part of the proceeds I put into a money market fund, and with the rest I bought some utility stocks and other securities offering high yields.

But my eye was also fixed on the DJIA's all-time high of 1051. As the market approached closer and closer to 1000, and looked as though it might be getting ready to make an assault on its previous high, I was ready to alter my strategy completely.

For a discussion of what to do when the DJIA is above 1050, turn now to Part II.

PART
II

8

A Major Bull Market Is Underway

If we look back we see that the ATS would have served us well during the past two decades. The stock market began a steady climb upward after hitting rock bottom following the Crash of 1929. It rose strongly for thirty years, first passing through 700 in 1961, then dropping back down to 550 before advancing strongly for the next three-and-a-half years, until it touched the magic 1000 level for the first time ever in the beginning of 1966.

From that point on the DJIA traded in a fairly narrow range, between 650 and 1000, until it made its historical high of 1051 in the opening days of 1973. Then came the monumental crash of 1974, which saw the DJIA plunge below 600 again, the first time it had been that low since 1962. The market got off to a good start during the first few trading sessions of 1975, soaring all the way back up to 850 by the end of the year. The year 1976 started with a bang as well. Within days the DJIA rocketed to 1000, and hovered at that level for the rest of the year. For the next three years, however, the trend was generally downward. The market kept on fading throughout 1977 and bottomed out at 750 by the beginning of the following year.

During the first quarter of 1978, after hovering at the 750 level for nearly three months, the market built up a head of steam again and rallied to 900, where it remained until September. Then came another big sell-off in early October and, within the space of a few short weeks, the DJIA bottomed out below 800. A few months later the DJIA shot back up to 900 again. In October 1979, exactly one year after the last major sell-off, as newspapers and magazines around the country carried stories warning us that we were approaching the fiftieth anniversary of the Crash of '29, the market collapsed once more.

December 1979 was another good time to load up on stocks again. The market got off to a roaring good start in January 1980, and continued strong for six solid weeks until the breathtaking crash in mid-February. This time the DJIA got as low as 740 before rallying all the way back up to 995, a run of over 250 points, by November.

As we look back over the charts, not only for the DJIA, but for the Standard & Poor 500, the New York Stock Exchange's Common Stock Index, the Over-the-Counter Industrial Average, and other common stock indicators, we see that the stock market went basically nowhere for the two decades beginning in 1960 and ending in 1980. For twenty long years, following a major bull market that lasted for almost thirty years, the DJIA ranged, for the most part, in a narrow band between 700 and 1000, except for a couple of brief instances when it dipped as low as 550 and spiked as high as 1051. When we factor in inflation for this two-decade-long stretch, we see that the stock market has been in a primary bear cycle during this period. A thousand on the DJIA today is equal to about 350 in 1968 dollars.

Had we utilized our ATS over the last twenty years, we can see that we would have been on the right side of the market all along. The signals told us to buy stocks in the early 1960s and sell them at the market peak in 1966. We would have loaded up again at the end of 1966, and gotten out of the market once more a year later. The signals said to buy again in early 1968 and sell off at the end of that year. In 1970 we would have been buyers in the earlier part of the year and remained long until the DJIA went over 900 again in 1971. At the end of 1971, when the DJIA dipped to 800, we would have been back in stocks once more, and we would have been selling off shares as the DJIA crossed 900, then 950, and eventually ran to 1051 in early 1973.

When the market started to slip during the first quarter of 1973, then kept on sliding until it dropped below 900, we would have liquidated our complete position, following the ATS, and been out well before the staggering collapse in 1974, which saw the averages fall below 600 for the first time in twelve years. As the market rebuilt itself in January 1975, the signals told us to start accumulating stocks again, and a new sell signal would not have been generated until the market returned to the 900–1000 range in 1976. As the market came below 900 in mid-1977, this would have triggered a new sell signal, and we would not have been buyers until the signals told us to start accumulating shares again December 1977–January 1978. A new sell signal flashed in September 1978, after the DJIA had rallied back over 900, only to be followed by another buy signal three months later as the year came to a close.

From there on in, the buy and sell signals were triggered much more frequently as the economy became stigmatized, with double-digit interest rates and inflation soaring above 18 percent. Until this time in history, interest rates and inflation played a relatively minor role, or perhaps we should say a less traumatic role, in determining our ATS. High interest rates did hurt the stock market in the past, most notably in 1974, but they were puny compared to the 17 percent yields available on six-month bank certificates in the opening months of 1980.

Between early 1978 and mid-1980, the DJIA jiggled sharply from 800 or lower to 900 or higher no less than four times. The cycles got narrower and tighter, taking weeks or months to complete themselves when, previously, they had lasted for months and years. Deciphering the ATS started to get a bit more tricky, since we had to keep a cautious eye simultaneously on the DJIA, inflation, yields on short-term securities, money supply figures, and other economic news. In the old days it was possible to buy stocks and hold them for months, even years at a time without having to worry about any sudden surprises; all of a sudden, in the closing years of the 1970s, we had to keep a close watch on the ATS at all times, or run the risk of suffering some dramatic consequences.

So while the ATS would have served us well for the past twenty years or longer—ever since the DJIA first entered its narrow trading band and embarked on a primary bear cycle—they have been especially critical during the past five or six years.

The question arises: What happens if the stock market breaks through the 1050 barrier, and keeps on advancing to new highs, 1200, 1300, and beyond? What happens to our ATS then?

Three years ago, in *The Optimist's Guide to Making Money in the 1980's,* I wrote:

> My own scenario . . . calls for a reversal in the misfortunes of the U.S. economy and dollar starting around 1982. At this point I think the American stock market will enter one of the strongest and best-sustained bull cycles in history. If this is true, then it is

reasonable to assume that the best place for growth investments in
the 1980's will, once again, be the stock market.

Since that was written, virtually every major brokerage firm on
Wall Street and many investment analysts, with the exception of
the perennial doomsday criers, have said essentially the same
thing. Donald T. Regan, chief executive officer of Merrill Lynch,
has been predicting 100-million-share days at press conferences
since 1979, and he has been readying his firm for the paper
crunch that will follow. Merrill Lynch analysts put out a strong
buy signal in the summer of 1980, even as the market was advancing 200 points from its low in March, and they were advising
their clients to load up on stocks for the major bull market ahead.
At Shearson Loeb Rhoades, the second largest brokerage firm in
the country, Jerry Rolfe and other technical and fundamental analysts were making the same projections. Robert Nurock, the top
analyst at Butcher, Singer, a regional firm headquartered in Philadelphia, has been talking about a long-term, primary bull market
for the past couple of years.
    Most of this optimism is based on the fact that, while other
investment vehicles have been increasing steadily in value for
quite some time, common stocks have failed to keep up with
inflation for two decades. Gold, diamonds, real estate, silver,
works of art, antiques, and other collectibles have all outper-
formed the stock market during this period. In the 1980s, the
argument goes, common stocks will once again be the best hedge
against inflation, since they are so undervalued now and have so
much room to move up.
    This line of reasoning is buttressed by another projection: that
the U.S. economy, and the value of the dollar, will strengthen
considerably throughout the 1980s. New tax cuts, particularly in
the area of depreciation for business to spur corporate investment, will pump a shot of adrenaline into the American economy.
Earnings will increase substantially, forcing the prices of common
shares that are currently selling at only 6 or 7 times current earnings to much higher levels. Tax breaks for individuals, most notably in the area of capital gains treatment and other investment
areas, will encourage investment in the stock market. Deregula-
tion of major segments of American industry will also make U.S.
corporations more competitive with foreign businesses. This, in
a nutshell, is the optimistic scenario, and so far the trend seems

to be holding in that direction, regardless of which political party controls the White House and the Congress.

"The stock market has risen in classic fashion in anticipation of the next major cyclical advance in corporate profits. Further enhancing the appeal of stocks has been the increasing political support for saving and investment incentives, a support which is essentially bipartisan. Finally, the secular bull market, driven by earnings and asset inflation, persists. We remain quite bullish in our investment approach," a Shearson report stated in August 1980.

Dr. John S. Lazar, professor of finance at the University of Hartford, was no less enthusiastic in his market letter. According to him, "It is axiomatic that the best investments are made in times when nobody wants to commit new funds. . . . Finding myself in a consensus of constructive market performance and commentary doesn't turn me to pessimism. A good Contrarian is a flexible one: one should not contradict trends for its own sake. . . . If you missed the early recovery of the market, don't spend time brooding over lost opportunities. Defense, energy, and capital equipment should be the growth industries of our future decade. We continue to favor equity commitments in these sectors."

At Bernstein-Macaulay, a money management firm that controls $1.5 billion in client funds, the outlook is equally bullish. According to a report written by Dr. Harold B. Ehrlich, chief executive officer of the firm, "Stock ownership has become fashionable again, if only because a great deal of money has been made in the market during the past five years. . . . Despite heavy purchases during 1979 and 1980, many investment managers do not have the equity portions of their portfolios up to guideline targets at a time when the market has been surging and clients have been urging them to buy. . . . The psychology of 'hedging against inflation' through the ownership of equities should remain a powerful force in the marketplace."

All of a sudden, an optimistic attitude vis-à-vis the stock market has become the majority position. A few short years ago a stock market bull was regarded as someone who was certifiably insane, along with people who still believed the earth was flat and the forests were filled with dragons. Only an incorrigible Contrarian maintained a rose-colored vision of the future of the stock market while everyone else was convinced the world was coming to an end.

Now the tide has turned. It is no longer any fun to be an out-of-step optimist as more and more people fall in line. The great temptation for perennial optimists, such as myself, is to quit the ranks and join the doomsday brigade, the legion of doom criers led by Howard Ruff, Harry Browne (who has lately become something of an optimist himself), and others who believe in loading up on gold, shotguns, and dried food, and running off to a cave somewhere. After all, wouldn't a true Contrarian regard all this recurrent optimism with suspicion, as a sign that it is time to change direction, since the majority of investors, professionals included, are wrong most of the time? Or does it behoove one to be "flexible" and not "contradict trends for its own sake," to use the words of Dr. Lazar?

Well, the main point here is not to prove who is right or wrong about the future, the pessimist or the optimist; our primary concern is to outline an investment strategy *so foolproof* that it really doesn't matter who is right and who is wrong. In Part I we developed a program, complete with Automatic Trigger Signals, to direct your investment capital under market conditions that have prevailed for the past twenty years. If those conditions continue to hold sway over the indefinite future, you *need not worry about anything else*. What follows will not concern you except, possibly, as a speculative exercise. But if conditions *do* change and the market keeps advancing to unprecedented new highs, then the following strategies will enable you to take advantage of them. Most important, these updated strategies will *insure you against loss* and help you reap substantial profits *whether the market rises or falls*.

Let's take a look now at some winning investment strategies in the event of a roaring bull market.

When the DJIA Is Above 1050

For the Conservative Investor

Toward the end of this book I have made a long list of stock recommendations, at suggested purchase prices, for when the DJIA is at the low end of the trading range it has occupied for the past twenty years. These stocks advanced well beyond the suggested purchase prices as the market moved from 740 to 995 by November 1980. As stated earlier, my strategy has been to sell off shares of individual stocks as they moved up in value, getting more heavily into a cash position as the DJIA gets closer to 1000. This strategy has worked well so far, and I have been able to buy many of the recommended stocks at the suggested purchase prices on various occasions over the years. As long as this twenty-year trading pattern persists, I highly recommend sticking to the strategy outlined so far, allowing the automatic trigger signals to tell you what to do under various market conditions.

The question now is: What should we do if the optimists are right and the stock market starts making new highs in the months and years ahead? Clearly a new strategy is called for under these circumstances.

If the DJIA closes above 1051, this will be our first definite sign that the long-awaited *primary bull market is finally underway.* The greatest danger at this point will *not* be getting whipsawed in a downdraft, but rather being left behind as stock market prices march off to higher and higher levels. If you fail to participate in the moves that lie ahead, you will miss the greatest opportunity for making profits that the decade will offer.

Does this mean simply rushing in and accumulating stocks at double and triple the prices I suggest at the end of this book?

Yes, but only *certain kinds* of stocks, and with an insurance policy built in to *protect you against any sharp declines* that may take place. The strategies we will discuss in the pages ahead are hedging strategies, designed to insure you against loss while you participate in a market that is moving to new highs.

Remember, the market can change direction at any time, and most likely will. No trend moves in a straight line, up or down; there are always corrections along the way, pullbacks, times when it appears that the trend has actually changed and a new cycle is underway. Be prepared for these corrections, but don't be trapped by them. Don't panic and abandon ship, and then be sorry as the market resumes its long climb up after stumbling for a while.

Nothing will kill off a bull market faster than sharply rising interest rates. Keep your eyes glued to the ATS, particularly interest rates, money supply figures, and inflation, as you pursue the updated strategies. If yields on treasury bills and other money market instruments rise into double digits and stay there for a while, you can expect a sharp setback in stock market prices. But, basically, a new market pattern will be developing once we cross the 1050 barrier, and the long-term trend over the next few years should be extremely bullish.

Now let's get down to some specifics.

BUY A STOCK, BUY A PUT

When you buy a stock at substantially higher prices than those I suggest at the end of the book, make sure you hedge yourself against loss through the use of options. Many people are afraid to get involved with options, figuring they are too complicated to understand properly.

But options, if they are used intelligently, can be an extremely conservative investment, and they can serve as an insurance policy against a major loss.

For the uninitiated, there are two types of options: *puts* and *calls*. When you buy a call you are buying the right to purchase 100 shares of a specific stock at a specific price before a specific date. For example, let's suppose that Polaroid is currently selling at $34 a share. You feel that the stock will move up past 35 within the next few months. In April you buy a Polaroid July 35. In this case, Polaroid is the underlying stock, 35 is the strike price, and the day in July when the option expires is the expiration date. The period covering the time you buy the call until it expires is the option life.

In the example above, you have until the expiration date to make your move. If Polaroid moves up past 35 to, say 38, you can buy 100 shares of Polaroid at the strike price, 35, and resell the shares immediately at the market price for a 3-point profit. Or you can sell your option, which will also have gone up in value. In reality, most people who buy options elect to sell them at a profit if they can, rather than buy the underlying stock. The reason for this is that they are looking for leverage. Options are relatively inexpensive compared to stocks. In our example, you might have paid 2 points ($200) for the option. If Polaroid makes 38, the option would be worth about 4 points, or $400, in which case you would have doubled your money. If you buy the stock itself for $3,500 and resell it for $3,800, the profit is $300, or less than 10 percent of your investment. So you can see why most individuals who buy options do not actually buy the underlying stock. By buying and selling the call options themselves, they are getting good leverage for relatively small amounts of money.

The other side of the coin is that the underlying stock may not go up at all. Or it may not go up far enough. Or fast enough. Polaroid could remain at 34 or it could go down. Then again, it may only go up to 34½, or it may not go up past 35 until August.

What happens then? If Polaroid does not go up far or fast enough, or if it goes down, your call option will decline in value. As you approach the expiration date, time literally begins to run out on you. You have to make your move within the life of the option. If you do not, then your calls will expire worthless and you will lose your entire investment.

The seller of a call, also known as an option writer, is on the other side of the fence. Let's assume that you own 500 shares of Polaroid, and that it is selling at $34 a share. You decide you would like to increase your income from the stock, so you write five Polaroid July 35s (one for each 100 shares). The call is worth 2 points or $200, which means you will receive $1,000 (less commissions). This money is called your option premium, and many shareholders regard it as extra dividend money.

If Polaroid goes up past 35 by expiration date, it can be called away from you at $35 a share. This is what you are selling when you write calls on stocks you own: the right for someone to call your stock away from you at the strike price if it goes up in value.

If your stock remains below 35, the buyer of the calls loses and you keep the $1,000 and your stock. You can then rewrite new options for October, bring in another $1,000 or so, and keep the game going until the new expiration date. You can keep the cash flow coming in as long as you manage to hold on to the stock. You don't have to lose your stock if you don't want to, of course. If Polaroid pushes beyond 35, you can buy back the calls you wrote at a higher price than you sold them for, in which case you will have lost money on the calls.

Puts are the opposite side of the options coin. When you buy a put you are buying the right to sell 100 shares of a specific stock at a specific price before a specific date. You buy puts in anticipation of lower prices, or to protect yourself against falling prices, in the underlying stock. So if Polaroid were currently selling at 37 and you thought it might fall below 35 within the next few months, you might buy one or five or ten Polaroid 35 puts expiring sometime in the future. If Polaroid falls to 32 before the expiration date, your puts will rise in value and you will be able to sell them for a profit. If you own Polaroid shares already and you buy puts with a 35 strike price, you have the right to sell your shares at 35 no matter how low the stock falls before the expiration date.

Naturally, if Polaroid remains above 35, or if it goes higher, your puts will expire worthless. The basic thing to keep in mind is that when you buy calls you will make money if the stock goes up, and if you buy puts you make money when the stock goes down. Buying puts is a safer way of going short on a stock, since your risk is limited to the price you paid for the puts, whereas when you short a stock your potential loss is virtually unlimited.

The seller, or writer, of put options is agreeing to buy the underlying stock at the strike price if it should fall below that price before the expiration date. So if you wrote or sold two Polaroid July 35s when Polaroid was at 37, you would have to buy 200 shares of Polaroid at $35 a share if the stock falls below that price. The buyer of the put has the right to sell or put the stock to you at the strike price, no matter how far down the stock goes before the expiration date. If Polaroid should remain above 35 through the life of the option, you get to keep the option premium without having to buy the stock or buy your puts back at a loss as the underlying stock falls in price.

If all this sounds rather complicated, remember there are only two kinds of options—puts and calls—and only two things you can do with them—buy them or sell them. Everything else follows from these transactions, and the consequences should become a bit clearer as we look at some actual examples.

Getting back to the strategy under discussion, in this particular case we are going to buy a stock high as the market moves to higher and higher ground, but we are also going to buy puts on the stock to protect ourselves on the downside. There are two basic rules to keep in mind when you are buying stocks above the suggested purchase prices:

1. Buy only those stocks that have listed puts and calls on them. I have included a complete list of these stocks, along with the exchanges they are traded on and their monthly expiration cycles, in Chapter Ten.

2. Try to zero in on stocks that have not participated fully in the latest bull market, that is, those stocks with listed puts and calls that have not risen substantially beyond my suggested purchase prices.

If you stick to these basic rules, you will minimize your risk and increase your chances for reaping future profits. Now, let's look at some specific examples.

In the summer rally of 1980, Kennecott, Occidental Petroleum, Bally Manufacturing, and Northwest Industries were four issues, all of them with listed puts and calls, that did not participate nearly as well as some other stocks. Kennecott was trading around 28, up only a few points from my buying range of 22–25; Occidental at 27½, up about 5 points from my suggested buying range of 19–22; Northwest Industries at 31½, 5 points above my range of 23–26; and Bally, which I usually don't recommend at all since it pays a puny dividend, seemed to me especially undervalued at 26½.

Let's assume now that the DJIA has just broken the 1050 barrier and that these four stocks are available at the above market prices. The downside risk on each stock runs to about 5 to 7 points apiece if the market should really take a beating and get hammered down below 800 again. Yet I would like to participate in future market advances if stocks continue to rally strongly. The last thing I want is to get left on the sidelines, missing what could be one of the roaringest bull markets in history.

What do I do?

One thing I can do is adopt a "buy a stock, buy a put" strategy.

Puts with a strike price of 25, expiring approximately three months out, could be bought for about three-quarters of a point, or $75 including commissions, on Kennecott, Occidental, and Bally; puts with a 30 strike price with a similar option life could be had for roughly the same price on Northwest Industries. So here's what we do:

Transaction	Cost
Buy 300 KN (Kennecott) @ 28	$ 8,400
Buy 3 KN 25 puts	225
Buy 300 OXY (Occidental Petroleum) @ 27½	8,250
Buy 3 OXY 25 puts	225
Buy 300 BLY (Bally) @ 26½	7,950
Buy 3 BLY 25 puts	300
Buy 300 NWT (Northwest Industries) @ 31½	9,450
Buy 3 NWT 30 puts	300
Total cost of stocks	$34,050
Total cost of puts	$ 1,050

We have made an investment of a little more than $34,000 in stocks, and paid a bit more than $1,000 for an insurance premium. There are only three things that can happen from this point on: the stocks we bought will stay where they are, go down, or go up.

Given the kind of volatility we have gotten accustomed to lately, it is most unlikely that our stocks will simply stay where they are. If they do, however, we have to buy new puts for the next three-month period to keep our insurance policy in effect. The dividends we bring in from the stocks will more than offset the cost of the puts, so in reality the insurance policy costs us nothing, and we will actually have a small return on our equities as we hold them for a potential future advance. If the stocks should hover at these levels for any period of time, I would suggest writing calls on them to increase our income (more on this a bit later).

If the stocks fall in value, there are two things we can do. We can exercise our puts, that is, sell the stocks we bought at the strike prices, thereby cutting our losses and warding off any future disaster. The most we can lose on KN is 3 points, on OXY 2½ points, on BLY 1½ points, and on NWT 1½ points. We will also lose the money we paid for the puts, less any dividends we may have received on the stocks. Remember, the strategy we have adopted here is one that enables us to minimize our losses in the event the market takes a nosedive after we have gotten in at a high level.

We do not have to exercise our puts, however, if our stocks fall in price. We also have the option of holding on to our stocks for the long run, buying additional shares as they fall in price to average down our cost, and *taking a profit on the puts.* As our stocks fall in value, our puts will be going up. If KN drops from 28 to 23, we will be down 5 points on paper on the stock, but our puts will be worth approximately 3 points, or $900, nearly $700 above our $225 purchase price. The same is true for all the other puts we bought. When the stock market finally bottoms out, these stocks will be back within my original buying range again, and we can buy additional shares at lower prices and ride them back up during the next bull market.

Under most circumstances, this is the strategy I would prefer myself. Since I have seen the market fluctuate so sharply over the years, I have confidence that the stocks we bought will eventually advance to the prices I paid for them and beyond. I would rather lock in my profits on the puts, hang on to the stocks, collect my quarterly dividends, and perhaps write some calls against the stocks to increase my income as I wait for the next bull cycle to begin.

The one thing that could change this strategy faster than any-thing else is sharply rising interest rates. If you are buying stocks high and interest rate yields on treasury bills and six-month bank certificates suddenly start jumping into the teens, *be prepared for a major crash ahead.* Take your small losses and bail out in a hurry. You can always buy stocks again when the dust settles and the market hits bottom; in other words, when the *ATS tell you to.*

The best possible scenario that can evolve is the third one: the bull market continues and these stocks keep rising in value. In this instance we will have paid the premium on our insurance policy, which will more than be offset by the dividends from the stocks, and we can simply sit back and watch our stocks keep climbing to higher and higher ground. If the stocks go up 10 or 20 points from our purchase prices, we can *buy new puts at higher strike prices* to lock in our gain on paper.

For example, if KN rises to 47, we can buy 45 puts to make sure that, no matter how low the stock drops in a falling market, we will never get less than $45 for it during the life of the option.

The "buy a stock, buy a put" strategy allows you to cut your losses in the face of impending disaster, to take profits on your puts while the market whipsaws up and down (and eventually get profits on your stocks as well), or simply sit back comfortably as your gains keep growing and lock in large profits at higher and higher levels.

Let's talk now about a variation on this strategy that costs a bit more up front, but provides you with a little more flexibility.

BUY A STOCK, BUY TWO PUTS

For additional flexibility, consider buying two puts instead of one for every 100 shares you own. We'll look at the numbers first, and then discuss possible scenarios.

Transaction	Cost
Buy 300 KN @ 28	$ 8,400
Buy 6 KN 25 puts	450
Buy 300 OXY @ 27½	8,250
Buy 6 OXY 25 puts	450
Buy 300 BLY @ 26½	7,950
Buy 6 BLY 25 puts	600
Buy 300 NWT @ 31½	9,450
Buy 6 NWT 30 puts	600
Total cost of stocks	$34,050
Total cost of puts	$ 2,100

In this situation, we have spent an extra thousand dollars or so on puts, but we have what amounts to the best of all possible worlds; this is what we are paying for.

Let's assume that, after setting up this portfolio, it turns out that we were monumentally wrong. Instead of being on the verge of the greatest bull market in stock market history, stocks start plummeting rapidly. What should we do?

We'll use Bally this time as an example. Let's say it turns out that the bloom is finally off the rose forever as far as casino gambling is concerned. Bally starts plunging and keeps on falling all the way down to 14, a new low for the stock since it began its long climb of a few years ago, before the splits. The proper course of action is as follows:

1. Exercise three BLY puts and sell your shares at 25.
2. Ride out the long decline and sell your remaining puts, which would be worth about 15 points each, before expiration date.

Sell 3 BLY 25 puts @ 15	Proceeds are	$4,500
Sell 300 BLY @ 25	Loss on stock	450
	Cost of puts	600
	Total profit	$3,450

I've picked a dramatic example here to drive home the point, but the principle is the same with all the stocks we own. Add the cost of your puts to the loss you would be taking on the stock, then subtract this figure from the proceeds you would be getting on the sale of your free puts (those which do not serve as an insurance policy). The result is your overall profit. You may have collected some dividends as well, depending on the time of your purchases, which helps to sweeten the pot.

If the market does keep on moving ahead to higher levels, you can sit back and watch your profits grow, as in the first strategy, the only difference being that here your start-up costs were higher. Your profits will be diminished by the cost of the extra puts.

If you feel more comfortable knowing that you can bail out of your stocks with a relatively small loss *and* profit in a down market with extra puts, then you should spend the extra money up front and buy two puts for every 100 shares you own.

BUY A STOCK, BUY A PUT, SELL A CALL

One way to take out an insurance policy on your stocks without paying anything, and actually making a few dollars on the deal, is to sell or write calls on the stocks you own in addition to buying the puts.

The figures will break down roughly as follows.

Transaction	Cost	Proceeds
Buy 300 KN @ 28	$ 8,400	
Buy 3 KN 25 puts	225	
Sell 3 KN 30 calls, going out to the next expiration date*		$ 600
Buy 300 OXY @ 27½	8,250	
Buy 3 OXY 25 puts	225	
Sell 3 OXY 30 calls, going out to the next expiration date		600
Buy 300 BLY @ 26½	7,950	
Buy 3 BLY 25 puts	300	
Sell 3 BLY 30 calls, going to the next expiration date		525
Buy 300 NWT @ 31½	9,450	
Buy 3 NWT 30 puts	300	
Sell 3 NWT 35 calls, going out to the next expiration date		450
Total cost of stocks	$34,050	
Total cost of puts	$ 1,050	
Total proceeds		$2,175
Total cost	$32,925	

In this situation, call premiums will be worth much more than put premiums, since put premiums shrink in value and call premiums become overpriced in a bull market. So we have bought insurance on our stocks and reaped a $1,125 profit on the options—which, when added to the dividends we will be receiving on our stocks, increases our overall return.

The most unlikely scenario is that the stocks will simply stay at the same prices indefinitely. If this should happen, we can keep rewriting new calls as the old ones expire, and buying additional puts for insurance. But markets never remain stagnant for more than brief periods at a time. Sooner or later we will get a sharp move either up or down, and then it will be time to take some action.

If our stocks drop below the strike price on the puts, we have the same choice to make that we did in our "buy a stock, buy a put" strategy. We can either exercise the puts and take a small loss on the stocks, in this case a smaller loss since we have brought in some money from our calls, or hold the stocks and sell the puts for a profit.

* Options expire in three-month cycles (e.g., January/April/July/October). See Chapter Ten for a list of stocks with options and their expiration cycles.

If we take the first action, we also have to buy back our calls, which will be virtually worthless—otherwise we run the risk of watching the stocks go back up to a point where they will be called away from us, forcing us to buy additional shares at a much higher price than we originally paid. I prefer the second course of action myself—sell the puts for a profit, hold the stock, perhaps buy more shares at lower prices, and wait for the next bull market to drive them back up in value.

Finally, our stocks may keep on rising in price after we set up our portfolio. If the stocks move above the strike prices on the calls, we run the risk of having them called away at the strike prices. For example, we paid 31½ for NWT. The puts cost us $300 and we brought in $450 for writing the calls, a profit of $150. If the stock jumps above the strike price on the call, which is 35, the stock can be called away from us at $35 a share even though it may rise, perhaps, to $40 or more. If we allow this to happen, we will have realized a profit of 3½ points on the stock, or $1,050 for 300 shares, in addition to the $150 option profit.

Profit on options		$ 150
Sell 300 NWT @ 35	$10,500	
Buy 300 NWT @ 31¼	9,450	
Profit on stock		1,050
	Total profit	$1,200

This represents a substantial return on an investment of a little more than $9,000 for a period of a few months. However, we will also have lost the opportunity to participate in a major upward move in the stock if the DJIA keeps on soaring to higher and higher levels. To maintain our position in the stock, and make sure it is not called away from us, we may choose to take the following action. Let's assume that NWT jumps to 38 and we decide we want to keep it. We can:

1. Buy back our NWT 35 calls at a loss;
2. Buy NWT 35 puts to lock in a 3½ point profit on the stock;
3. Write NWT 40 calls to bring in new money.

Here's how our position looks:

Paper profit of 6½ points on NWT		$1,950
Buy 3 NWT 35 calls for a loss of	$ 650	
Buy 3 NWT 35 puts for a total cost of	600	
Sell 3 NWT 40 calls for total cash proceeds		900
Total losses and cost of puts	$1,250	
Total profits and proceeds		$2,850
Net gain		$1,600

At this point we are in precisely the same situation we started out in, except that we have locked in profits and hedged our position at a higher level. While I have not factored commissions into these transactions, neither have I added in the cash flow from dividends, which would be substantially higher.

By utilizing the strategies we have discussed so far, we are adopting extremely conservative techniques for hedging ourselves when we buy stocks at relatively high prices after a bull market has gotten underway.

For the Aggressive Risk-Taker

BUY A CALL, BUY A PUT

A riskier approach to making profits in volatile markets, but one that requires less capital up front and allows you to make money whether the market goes *up or down,* is to buy a spread.

If the market has been swinging wildly, advancing to higher levels with sharp corrections or pullbacks along the way, you might consider buying calls and puts simultaneously, providing you don't mind risking your entire investment. Remember, when you buy calls you will make money if the underlying stock moves up within the life of the option, and when you buy puts the reverse is true—you profit when the underlying stock falls in price.

When you buy a spread on a stock, make sure the underlying stock is a volatile one, that is, one that fluctuates rapidly in a broad trading range. The worst thing that can happen when you own both puts and calls on a stock is for it to just sit there and do nothing during the life of the options. If that happens, both your puts and your calls will expire worthless and you will have lost your entire investment.

For example, let's say that Bally has been swinging wildly between 15 and 36 during the past few months. Currently the stock is trading around 28 and you are not quite sure which way the next move will be. So you decide to buy both puts and calls on it in order to make money no matter which way it moves.

Transaction	Cost
Buy 5 BLY 30 calls	$1,000
Buy 5 BLY 25 puts	600
Total cost	$1,600

If Bally ranges between 25 and 30 for the next few months until your options expire, you will wind up losing your entire $1,600 investment. But if the stock swings sharply in either direction, as it had in the past, you will make money on either the put or call side of the spread.

Should the stock rise sharply into the mid-30s, your 30 calls will have appreciated considerably. With Bally at 35 and a month left before the calls expire, they would be worth about 8 points, or $800, each. Your puts, of course, would be worthless, but you would be able to sell the calls for a total of $4,000, for a profit of $2,400 on an investment of $1,600 over a short period of time. Not bad leverage, to say the least.

You will also make money if the stock declines sharply. Should Bally drop to 18 during the option life, your puts will be worth approximately 10 points, or $1,000, each, while your calls will be worthless. You will have a profit of $3,400 on your $1,600 investment over the same period.

Lesser swings in the stock will provide you with smaller profits, of course. And remember, no movement at all will result in the loss of all or part of your investment. There are two things you should keep in mind if you decide to buy options rather than the actual stock itself:

1. Nine out of ten people who buy options for speculation rather than as a hedge lose money;

2. The one out of ten who makes money buying options usually does so within the first few weeks, and does not wait, hoping for the move he is looking for, until the options expire.

If you do decide to gamble with the relatively small sum required to buy options, instead of committing the larger amount needed to buy stocks, do not wait until the last minute to get out. If you do not get the move you are looking for in the underlying stock within the first few weeks, cut your loss and get out early. The longer you wait, the more time begins to work against you. The value of your options begins to dwindle sharply the closer you get to expiration date.

BUY A STOCK, BUY A PUT, SELL TWO CALLS

This is a variation on the "buy a stock, buy a put, sell a call" strategy. In this case, however, we are assuming greater risk by writing or selling more calls than we own stock for. When you do this it is sometimes referred to as *ratio writing*. Let's look at the numbers first, and then discuss the consequences.

Transaction	Cost	Proceeds
Buy 300 KN @ 28	$ 8,400	
Buy 3 KN 25 puts	225	
Sell 6 KN 30 calls		$1,200
Buy 300 OXY @ 27½	8,250	
Buy 3 OXY 25 puts	225	
Sell 6 OXY 30 calls		1,200
Buy 300 BLY @ 26½	7,950	
Buy 3 BLY 25 puts	300	
Sell 6 BLY 30 calls		1,050
Buy 300 NWT @ 31½	9,450	
Buy 3 NWT 30 puts	300	
Sell 6 NWT 35 calls		900
Total cost of stocks	$34,050	
Total cost of puts	$ 1,050	
Total proceeds		$4,350
Total cost	$30,750	

By using the technique of ratio writing, we have paid only $30,750 for over $34,000 worth of stock, and we are fully hedged on the downside against a big loss. Everything I said about possible scenarios in the "buy a stock, buy a put, sell a call" strategy applies here, with one major exception. If our stocks rise sharply in a continuing bull market, we run the risk of having not only the shares we own called away from us at the strike price of the calls, but an additional 300 shares that we *do not own.*

This means that either we will have to buy back three of the six call options we sold at a loss, or else we will have to buy 300 shares more of each, which we will also be taking a loss on. This latter could be a disaster which is to be avoided at any cost.

If you do decide to take advantage of ratio writing to bring in extra money when you are setting up your portfolio, be prepared to buy back your uncovered calls at a loss if your stocks start moving above the call strike price. This strategy works best when your stocks go up a little higher, but stay below the call strike prices until the options expire.

BUY A STOCK, SELL A CALL, SELL A PUT

In the event that you would like to bring in extra money and are willing to do without the insurance policy altogether, you could consider buying stock, selling calls, and selling puts instead of buying them. Selling or writing puts is a bullish strategy, to be undertaken when you are fairly sure your stocks will not decline in value, or when you do not mind buying additional shares at lower prices in anticipation of an upswing later on. Here's how it looks.

Transaction	Cost	Proceeds
Buy 300 KN @ 28	$ 8,400	
Sell 3 KN 25 puts		$225
Sell 3 KN 30 calls		600
Buy 300 OXY @ 27½	8,250	
Sell 3 OXY 25 puts		225
Sell 3 OXY 30 calls		600
Buy 300 BLY @ 26½	7,950	
Sell 3 BLY 25 puts		300
Sell 3 BLY 30 calls		525
Buy 300 NWT @ 31½	9,450	
Sell 3 NWT 30 puts		300
Sell 3 NWT 35 calls		450
Total cost of stocks	$34,050	
Total proceeds		$3,225

We have brought in over $3,000 in proceeds while putting up a little over $30,000 for $34,000 worth of stock, an instant return of about 10 percent on our investment. The best possible thing that can happen here is that our stocks keep on going up, since we have no downside protection, no insurance policy against a large loss.

If the stocks do keep on rising, our strategy would be the same as with our "buy a stock, buy a put, sell a call" portfolio. We can either allow the stocks to be called away from us at the call strike prices, in which case we will have a decent profit on the stocks in addition to the proceeds from selling the options; or else we can buy back the calls at a loss, hang on to the stock, and sell new puts and calls at higher strike prices if we choose. This way we will have a paper profit on our stocks and will be bringing in new proceeds from the new options.

The second-best thing that can happen is for our stocks to stay where they are, moving neither up nor down. In this scenario we would wait for the puts and calls we wrote to expire, then do it all over again for the next three-month period, generating another 10 percent return or thereabouts on our original investment.

The final scenario, and the worst one, is that the market turns against us and our stocks go down in value. In this event, we have no insurance policy to protect ourselves against a possible big loss, and we may also be forced to buy additional shares of stock at the put strike prices. Let's suppose that KN drops to 23 before the options expire. We have sold three KN puts, which gives someone the right to put, or sell, 300 shares of KN to us at $25 a share, no matter how low the stock drops.

What should we do if the market turns against us and heads south for the season?

My own strategy would be to *buy back* the puts at a loss and wait for the market to settle before buying additional stock. This means buying back three KN 25 puts as soon as the stock dips below $25 a share and/or as soon as the puts have doubled in value from our original cost. When we sold them we brought $225 in proceeds into our portfolio. The cost of buying them back is approximately $450. The entire position on KN now looks like this:

Transaction	Cost	Proceeds
Buy 300 KN @ 28	$8,400	
Sell 3 KN 25 puts		$225
Sell 3 KN 30 calls		600
Buy back 3 KN 25 puts	450	
Total cost	$8,850	
Total proceeds		$825

We have lowered our overall return on KN by buying back the puts, and we are also down a few points on the stock, but I would rather cut my losses early when the market turns against me than expose myself to even greater risk if the market keeps on falling. Eventually the sell-off will end and KN will bottom out, probably somewhere around $22 or $23 a share if we use its trading range of the past few years as a guide.

At that level, I would probably buy additional shares of KN to average down my overall cost, and *sell* KN 25 calls and KN 20 puts against these new shares. Remember, this is a *bullish* strategy, which works well in a flat or a rising market. When the market turns against you, *cut your losses early;* when the market bottoms out and begins to rise again, *start the process all over again.*

BUY TREASURY BILLS, SELL PUTS

The last strategy we will discuss here is an extremely sophisticated technique that provides you with the utmost in *safety;* you are actually *getting paid* while you wait to buy stocks. The best times to utilize this strategy are after a big sell-off when the market has bottomed out, and in the midst of a bull market when stocks are moving up. Do not use it when stocks are dropping and look as though they have a bit further to go. The only one who will be unhappy with this program, by the way, is your stockbroker, who makes little or no commission on treasury bills, and less commission on selling options than he would if you simply bought stocks from him.

The portfolio would be set up in the following manner:

Transaction	Cost	Proceeds
Buy $30,000 worth of 3-month treasury bills	Approximately $29,400 (depending on interest rates)	$600 (discounted interest)
Sell 3 KN 25 puts, expiring around the time the T-bills are due		225
Sell 3 OXY 25 puts		225
Sell 3 BLY 25 puts		300
Sell 3 NWT 30 puts		300
Total cost	$29,400	
Total proceeds		$1,650

Here we have earned $1,650 over three months on an investment of $29,400, for an annualized return of 22.5 percent. So far so good. What are the possible scenarios?

If the stocks remain at the same price, or do not drop below the put strike prices, we can keep on repeating the procedure every three months, rolling over our treasury bills into new three-month bills, and writing new put options. By doing this indefinitely, we can generate a return of 20 to 25 percent a year without assuming any risk.

If the stocks go up, the situation is basically the same, the only difference being that we will be selling puts with higher and higher strike prices as the bull market continues. We cannot get rich with this strategy, cannot participate fully if the DJIA and other indicators keep climbing to unprecedented heights. But neither are we taking any great risk, and a 22 percent return is pretty healthy for a relatively riskless investment strategy.

Alas, no rally continues forever. Sooner or later stocks will pull back as profit-taking sets in, interest rates move significantly higher, or inflation gets out of hand, or for some other reason not immediately discernible. When this happens, when stocks move down below the strike prices of the puts you sold, then you will be forced to buy the stocks at the strike prices in a falling market, or else, to avoid having to do so, you will have to buy back the puts you wrote at a loss.

The decision you make at this point depends on how comfortable you feel buying stocks at levels higher than their current market price. For instance, if OXY drops to 23 or 22, you will have to pay $25 a share for it. If you decide to do so, you will of course have to let your treasury bills mature and use the cash to pay for the stock, unless you have other funds you want to use. Using this same example, if you do decide to buy OXY at 25 when it is selling at 23, I would suggest buying OXY 20 puts to cover your downside in the event of a further decline, and perhaps writing OXY 25 calls to bring in extra money and help your cash flow situation.

Again, this is a relatively conservative strategy which works best in a flat or rising market.

We have looked at some hedging techniques to protect yourself when you are buying stocks above the prices I suggest when the DJIA is below 1050. We have also discussed some other strategies involving a higher level of risk, but with potentially greater rewards.

The strategy you opt for depends on your own personal chemistry. How much risk can you live with? Can you sleep nights knowing you are not fully hedged, owning stocks that are double and triple the price of their previous lows?

If the answer is no, then adopt the simplest strategy of buying a stock and buying a put to insure yourself on the downside, or, perhaps, of rolling over treasury bills and selling puts. If you don't mind a bit more risk, and you understand the consequences of the more sophisticated strategies we discussed, then you might try ratio writing or selling puts and calls simultaneously when you purchase stocks. These techniques require more careful monitoring, so you will have to spend a little more time, watching your positions like a hawk to make sure you don't get any unpleasant surprises.

The possibilities with options, the variations on bull spreads, bear spreads, calendar spreads, and so on, are virtually endless. The more sophisticated the strategy you adopt, the greater the degree of understanding and amount of time required to monitor your portfolio. It is safe to say that fully 95 percent or more of the brokers you will be working with do not understand the options market beyond the rudimentary level. When they get beyond buying puts or calls for speculation, or writing covered calls to bring in additional income, they are as lost as the most innocent neophyte. The options market is relatively new, and most stockbrokers, particularly those who started in the business before

1975, were not even required to know the options market in order to get their licenses.

So remember, if you adopt any of the strategies we have discussed in the preceding pages, chances are you will be almost entirely on your own. Don't expect your broker to watch over your positions and notify you when appropriate changes are called for. It will be up to you to make sure you do not have stock put to you when you don't want to buy it, or have stock called away that you don't already own.

The options market can be fun, and it can provide the more sophisticated investor with extra profits as well as a hedge against potential loss when it is used intelligently. If you decide to take the time to educate yourself on how it works, it can be a rewarding experience. If you do not have the time and inclination to do so, then keep it simple. Buy a stock and buy a put when the market is high, and go to sleep at night knowing that you are insured against disaster if your stocks suddenly fall out of bed. If that primary bull market does materialize over the months and years ahead, you will be able to participate knowing that, for a few extra dollars, you have limited your risk.

10

Stocks with Listed Puts and Calls

As I mentioned earlier, when the DJIA is soaring to new highs and you are buying stocks above my suggested buying range, stick to issues with listed puts and calls so that you can hedge yourself properly. Following is a list of those stocks, along with the exchanges their options are traded on, and their expiration cycles.

Company: Abbott Labs
Symbol: ABT
Exchange: Philadelphia
Cycle: Feb/May/Aug/Nov

Company: ABC
Symbol: ABC
Exchange: Pacific
Cycle: Feb/May/Aug/Nov

Company: Aetna Life
Symbol: AET
Exchange: American
Cycle: Jan/Apr/Jul/Oct

Company: Allied Chemical
Symbol: ACD
Exchange: Philadelphia
Cycle: Jan/Apr/Jul/Oct

Company: Allis-Chalmers
Symbol: AH
Exchange: Philadelphia
Cycle: Jan/Apr/Jul/Oct

Company: Amax
Symbol: AMX
Exchange: American
Cycle: Mar/Jun/Sep/Dec

Company: Amerada Hess
Symbol: AHC
Exchange: Philadelphia
Cycle: Feb/May/Aug/Nov

Company: American Cyanamid
Symbol: ACY
Exchange: American
Cycle: Jan/Apr/Jul/Oct

Company: American Express
Symbol: AXP
Exchange: American
Cycle: Jan/Apr/Jul/Oct

Company: Anheuser-Busch
Symbol: BUD
Exchange: Philadelphia
Cycle: Mar/Jun/Sep/Dec

Company: ASA Ltd.
Symbol: ASA
Exchange: American
Cycle: Feb/May/Aug/Nov

Company: Asarco
Symbol: AR
Exchange: American
Cycle: Mar/Jun/Sep/Dec

Company: Ashland Oil
Symbol: ASH
Exchange: Philadelphia
Cycle: Jan/Apr/Jul/Oct

Company: Atlantic Richfield
Symbol: ARC
Exchange: Chicago
Cycle: Jan/Apr/Jul/Oct

Company: Avnet
Symbol: AVT
Exchange: American
Cycle: Feb/May/Aug/Nov

Company: Avon
Symbol: AVP
Exchange: Chicago
Cycle: Jan/Apr/Jul/Oct

Company: Baker
Symbol: BKO
Exchange: Pacific
Cycle: Mar/Jun/Sep/Dec

Company: Bally
Symbol: BLY
Exchange: Chicago, American
Cycle: Feb/May/Aug/Nov

Company: Bausch & Lomb
Symbol: BOL
Exchange: American
Cycle: Jan/Apr/Jul/Oct

Company: Boeing
Symbol: BA
Exchange: Chicago
Cycle: Feb/May/Aug/Nov

Company: Bristol Myers
Symbol: BMY
Exchange: Chicago
Cycle: Mar/Jun/Sep/Dec

Company: Burroughs
Symbol: BGH
Exchange: American, Chicago
Cycle: Jan/Apr/Jul/Oct

Company: Caesar's World
Symbol: CAW
Exchange: Philadelphia
Cycle: Feb/May/Aug/Nov

Company: Charter
Symbol: CHR
Exchange: Philadelphia
Cycle: Mar/Jun/Sep/Dec

Company: Chase Manhattan
Symbol: CMB
Exchange: American
Cycle: Mar/Jun/Sep/Dec

Company: Cities Service
Symbol: CS
Exchange: Philadelphia
Cycle: Mar/Jun/Sep/Dec

Company: City Investing
Symbol: CNV
Exchange: Philadelphia
Cycle: Jan/Apr/Jul/Oct

Company: Coastal Corp.
Symbol: CGP
Exchange: American, Chicago
Cycle: Mar/Jun/Sep/Dec

Company: Comsat
Symbol: CQ
Exchange: Philadelphia
Cycle: Jan/Apr/Jul/Oct

Company: Conoco
Symbol: CLL
Exchange: Philadelphia
Cycle: Jan/Apr/Jul/Oct

Company: Control Data
Symbol: CDA
Exchange: Chicago
Cycle: Feb/May/Aug/Nov

Company: Corning Glass
Symbol: GLW
Exchange: Chicago
Cycle: Mar/Jun/Sep/Dec

Company: Deere & Co.
Symbol: DE
Exchange: American
Cycle: Mar/Jun/Sep/Dec

Company: Diamond Shamrock
Symbol: DIA
Exchange: Pacific
Cycle: Jan/Apr/Jul/Oct

Company: Digital Equipment
Symbol: DEC
Exchange: American, Chicago
Cycle: Jan/Apr/Jul/Oct

Company: Disney
Symbol: DIS
Exchange: American, Chicago
Cycle: Jan/Apr/Jul/Oct

Company: Dr. Pepper
Symbol: DOC
Exchange: American
Cycle: Feb/May/Aug/Nov

Company: Dow Chemical
Symbol: DOW
Exchange: Chicago
Cycle: Mar/Jun/Sep/Dec

Company: Dresser
Symbol: DI
Exchange: Philadelphia
Cycle: Jan/Apr/Jul/Oct

Company: Dupont
Symbol: DD
Exchange: American, Chicago
Cycle: Jan/Apr/Jul/Oct

Company: Eastern Gas
Symbol: EFU
Exchange: Philadelphia
Cycle: Jan/Apr/Jul/Oct

Company: Eastman Kodak
Symbol: EK
Exchange: Chicago
Cycle: Jan/Apr/Jul/Oct

Company: EG&G
Symbol: EGG
Exchange: Philadelphia
Cycle: Mar/Jun/Sep/Dec

Company: El Paso
Symbol: ELG
Exchange: American
Cycle: Feb/May/Aug/Nov

Company: Englehard
Symbol: ENG
Exchange: Philadelphia
Cycle: Jan/Apr/Jul/Oct

Company: Esmark
Symbol: ESM
Exchange: Chicago
Cycle: Mar/Jun/Sep/Dec

Company: Exxon
Symbol: XON
Exchange: Chicago
Cycle: Jan/Apr/Jul/Oct

Company: Federal Express
Symbol: FDX
Exchange: Chicago
Cycle: Jan/Apr/Jul/Oct

Company: First Chaifer Financial
Symbol: FCF
Exchange: American
Cycle: Jan/Apr/Jul/Oct

Company: Fluor
Symbol: FLR
Exchange: Chicago
Cycle: Jan/Apr/Jul/Oct

Company: Freeport Minerals
Symbol: FT
Exchange: Chicago
Cycle: Mar/Jun/Sep/Dec

Company: General Dynamics
Symbol: GD
Exchange: Chicago
Cycle: Feb/May/Aug/Nov

Company: General Electric
Symbol: GE
Exchange: Chicago
Cycle: Mar/Jun/Sep/Dec

Company: General Instrument
Symbol: GRL
Exchange: Philadelphia
Cycle: Mar/Jun/Sep/Dec

Company: General Motors
Symbol: GM
Exchange: Chicago
Cycle: Mar/Jun/Sep/Dec

Company: Georgia Pacific
Symbol: GP
Exchange: Philadelphia
Cycle: Jan/Apr/Jul/Oct

Company: Gulf Oil
Symbol: GO
Exchange: American
Cycle: Jan/Apr/Jul/Oct

Company: Halliburton
Symbol: HAL
Exchange: Chicago
Cycle: Jan/Apr/Jul/Oct

Company: Heublein
Symbol: HBL
Exchange: Pacific
Cycle: Feb/May/Aug/Nov

Company: Hewlett Packard
Symbol: HWP
Exchange: Chicago
Cycle: Feb/May/Aug/Nov

Company: Hilton
Symbol: HLT
Exchange: Pacific
Cycle: Feb/May/Aug/Nov

Company: Homestake Mines
Symbol: HM
Exchange: Chicago
Cycle: Jan/Apr/Jul/Oct

Company: Honeywell
Symbol: HON
Exchange: Chicago
Cycle: Feb/May/Aug/Nov

Company: Houston Oil
Symbol: HOI
Exchange: Chicago, Pacific
Cycle: Jan/Apr/Jul/Oct

Company: Hughes Tool
Symbol: HT
Exchange: Chicago
Cycle: Mar/Jun/Sep/Dec

Company: Hercules, Inc.
Symbol: HPC
Exchange: American
Cycle: Mar/Jun/Sep/Dec

Company: Household Finance
Symbol: HFC
Exchange: American
Cycle: Jan/Apr/Jul/Oct

Company: IBM
Symbol: IBM
Exchange: Chicago
Cycle: Jan/Apr/Jul/Oct

Company: Inexco Oil
Symbol: INX
Exchange: Philadelphia
Cycle: Feb/May/Aug/Nov

Company: International Harvester
Symbol: HR
Exchange: Chicago
Cycle: Jan/Apr/Jul/Oct

Company: Joy Mfg.
Symbol: JOY
Exchange: Philadelphia
Cycle: Feb/May/Aug/Nov

Company: Kennecott
Symbol: KN
Exchange: Chicago
Cycle: Mar/Jun/Sep/Dec

Company: Kerr McGee
Symbol: KMG
Exchange: Chicago
Cycle: Jan/Apr/Jul/Oct

Company: Lear Siegler
Symbol: LSI
Exchange: Philadelphia
Cycle: Mar/Jun/Sep/Dec

Company: Levi Strauss
Symbol: LVI
Exchange: Pacific
Cycle: Jan/Apr/Jul/Oct

Company: Litton
Symbol: LIT
Exchange: Chicago
Cycle: Mar/Jun/Sep/Dec

Company: Lockheed
Symbol: LK
Exchange: Pacific
Cycle: Mar/Jun/Sep/Dec

Company: Louisiana Land
Symbol: LLX
Exchange: Philadelphia
Cycle: Feb/May/Aug/Nov

Company: Mapco Inc.
Symbol: MDA
Exchange: Pacific
Cycle: Jan/Apr/Jul/Oct

Company: Marathon Oil
Symbol: MRO
Exchange: American
Cycle: Mar/Jun/Sep/Dec

Company: Marriott
Symbol: MHS
Exchange: Philadelphia
Cycle: Jan/Apr/Jul/Oct

Company: Martin Marietta
Symbol: ML
Exchange: Philadelphia
Cycle: Mar/Jun/Sep/Dec

Company: McDermott
Symbol: MDE
Exchange: Philadelphia
Cycle: Feb/May/Aug/Nov

Company: McDonnell Douglas
Symbol: MD
Exchange: Pacific
Cycle: Feb/May/Aug/Nov

Company: Merrill Lynch
Symbol: MER
Exchange: American, Chicago
Cycle: Jan/Apr/Jul/Oct

Company: Mesa Petroleum
Symbol: MSA
Exchange: American
Cycle: Jan/Apr/Jul/Oct

Company: Mobil Oil
Symbol: MOB
Exchange: Chicago
Cycle: Feb/May/Aug/Nov

Company: Motorola
Symbol: MOT
Exchange: American
Cycle: Jan/Apr/Jul/Oct

Company: National Cash Register
Symbol: NCR
Exchange: Chicago
Cycle: Mar/Jun/Sep/Dec

Company: National
  Semiconductor
Symbol: NSM
Exchange: Chicago, American
Cycle: Feb/May/Aug/Nov

Company: Natomas
Symbol: NOM
Exchange: American
Cycle: Mar/Jun/Sep/Dec

Company: Newmont Mining
Symbol: NEM
Exchange: Philadelphia
Cycle: Mar/Jun/Sep/Dec

Company: NL Industries
Symbol: NL
Exchange: Philadelphia
Cycle: Feb/May/Aug/Nov

Company: Northwest Industries
Symbol: NWT
Exchange: Chicago
Cycle: Mar/Jun/Sep/Dec

Company: Occidental Petroleum
Symbol: OXY
Exchange: Chicago
Cycle: Feb/May/Aug/Nov

Company: Owens Illinois
Symbol: OI
Exchange: Chicago
Cycle: Mar/Jun/Sep/Dec

Company: Penney (J. C.)
Symbol: JCP
Exchange: American
Cycle: Feb/May/Aug/Nov

Company: Perkin-Elmer
Symbol: PKN
Exchange: Pacific
Cycle: Mar/Jun/Sep/Dec

Company: Pfizer
Symbol: PFE
Exchange: American
Cycle: Mar/Jun/Sep/Dec

Company: Phillip Morris
Symbol: MO
Exchange: American
Cycle: Mar/Jun/Sep/Dec

Company: Phillips Petroleum
Symbol: P
Exchange: American
Cycle: Feb/May/Aug/Nov

Company: Pittston
Symbol: PCO
Exchange: Philadelphia
Cycle: Feb/May/Aug/Nov

Company: Polaroid
Symbol: PRD
Exchange: Chicago, Pacific
Cycle: Jan/Apr/Jul/Oct

Company: Prime Computer
Symbol: PRM
Exchange: American
Cycle: Mar/Jun/Sep/Dec

Company: Procter & Gamble
Symbol: PG
Exchange: American
Cycle: Jan/Apr/Jul/Oct

Company: Ralston Purina
Symbol: RAL
Exchange: Chicago
Cycle: Mar/Jun/Sep/Dec

Company: Resorts International
Symbol: RTA
Exchange: Pacific
Cycle: Jan/Apr/Jul/Oct

Company: Revlon
Symbol: REV
Exchange: Chicago
Cycle: Mar/Jun/Sep/Dec

Company: Reynolds Metals
Symbol: RLM
Exchange: Pacific
Cycle: Feb/May/Aug/Nov

Company: Rockwell International
Symbol: ROK
Exchange: Chicago
Cycle: Mar/Jun/Sep/Dec

Company: Santa Fe Industries
Symbol: SFF
Exchange: American
Cycle: Mar/Jun/Sep/Dec

Company: Santa Fe International
Symbol: SAF
Exchange: Pacific
Cycle: Jan/Apr/Jul/Oct

Company: Schering Plough
Symbol: SGP
Exchange: Pacific
Cycle: Feb/May/Aug/Nov

Company: Schlumberger
Symbol: SLB
Exchange: Chicago
Cycle: Feb/May/Aug/Nov

Company: Seaboard Coast
Symbol: SCI
Exchange: Philadelphia
Cycle: Jan/Apr/Jul/Oct

Company: Searle
Symbol: SRL
Exchange: American
Cycle: Feb/May/Aug/Nov

Company: Signal Company
Symbol: SGN
Exchange: Pacific
Cycle: Feb/May/Aug/Nov

Company: Standard Oil (Cal)
Symbol: SD
Exchange: American
Cycle: Mar/Jun/Sep/Dec

Company: Standard Oil (Ohio)
Symbol: SOH
Exchange: American
Cycle: Mar/Jun/Sep/Dec

Company: St. Joe Minerals
Symbol: SJO
Exchange: Philadelphia
Cycle: Mar/Jun/Sep/Dec

Company: Storage Technology
Symbol: STK
Exchange: Chicago
Cycle: Jan/Apr/Jul/Oct

Company: Sun Oil
Symbol: SUN
Exchange: Philadelphia
Cycle: Feb/May/Aug/Nov

Company: Superior Oil
Symbol: SOC
Exchange: Chicago
Cycle: Mar/Jun/Sep/Dec

Company: Syntex
Symbol: SYN
Exchange: Chicago
Cycle: Mar/Jun/Sep/Dec

Company: Tandy
Symbol: TAN
Exchange: American, Chicago
Cycle: Jan/Apr/Jul/Oct

Company: Tektronix
Symbol: TEK
Exchange: Chicago
Cycle: Mar/Jun/Sep/Dec

Company: Teledyne
Symbol: TDY
Exchange: Chicago, Pacific
Cycle: Jan/Apr/Jul/Oct

Company: Teleprompter
Symbol: TP
Exchange: American
Cycle: Mar/Jun/Sep/Dec

Company: Tenneco
Symbol: TGT
Exchange: American
Cycle: Feb/May/Aug/Nov

Company: Texaco
Symbol: TX
Exchange: American
Cycle: Jan/Apr/Jul/Oct

Company: Texas Oil & Gas
Symbol: TXO
Exchange: Philadelphia
Cycle: Mar/Jun/Sep/Dec

Company: Tiger International
Symbol: TGR
Exchange: American
Cycle: Feb/May/Aug/Nov

Company: Tosco
Symbol: TOS
Exchange: American
Cycle: Feb/May/Aug/Nov

Company: Travelers
Symbol: TIC
Exchange: Pacific
Cycle: Feb/May/Aug/Nov

Company: Union Carbide
Symbol: UK
Exchange: American
Cycle: Jan/Apr/Jul/Oct

Company: Union Oil
Symbol: UCL
Exchange: Pacific
Cycle: Jan/Apr/Jul/Oct

Company: Union Pacific
Symbol: UNP
Exchange: Philadelphia
Cycle: Feb/May/Aug/Nov

Company: U.S. Steel
Symbol: X
Exchange: American
Cycle: Jan/Apr/Jul/Oct

Company: Valero Energy
Symbol: VLO
Exchange: American
Cycle: Mar/Jun/Sep/Dec

Company: Warner
   Communications
Symbol: WCI
Exchange: Chicago
Cycle: Feb/May/Aug/Nov

Company: Warner Lambert
Symbol: WLA
Exchange: American
Cycle: Jan/Apr/Jul/Oct

Company: Westinghouse
Symbol: WX
Exchange: American
Cycle: Jan/Apr/Jul/Oct

Company: Williams Co.
Symbol: WMB
Exchange: Chicago
Cycle: Feb/May/Aug/Nov

Company: Xerox
Symbol: XRX
Exchange: Chicago, Pacific
Cycle: Jan/Apr/Jul/Oct

11

Tax Treatment of Options

PUTS

When you buy a put and hold it until it expires without exercising it, the premium or the amount you pay for the put is treated as a capital loss for the year the put expires. So for example, if you buy three KN 25 puts for $225 expiring in September of the current year, you will have a short-term loss of $225 for the year if you hold it and let it expire worthless.

If you sell the puts before they expire, the gain or loss is treated in the same fashion as a stock transaction. Since all listed puts expire in nine months or less, your gain or loss will be short-term. If you take a short-term loss on your puts, the loss will be fully deductible from your income subject to capital loss limitations. If you have a short-term gain, the gain is fully taxable as ordinary income.

When you exercise a put, the tax consequences get a trifle complicated. If you decide to exercise your puts, that is, sell the underlying stock at the strike price, the amount you paid for the puts can be deducted from the sale. Using the example above, let's say you exercise your three KN 25 puts and sell 300 shares of KN for $25 a share. Your proceeds are $7,500, less the $225 you paid for the puts. If you are taking a loss on the stock, the transaction is basically a simple one.

But if you should have a capital gain when you exercise the puts, the tax treatment gets a bit murky. Let's say you originally bought 300 KN at 20 and watched it rise to 27. To lock in a gain you bought three KN puts with a strike price of 25. When the stock fell below this price, you decided to exercise your puts and sell your 300 KN for $25 a share.

For tax purposes, the purchase of puts is treated as a short sale, and the exercise of the puts to sell the underlying security is ordinarily considered to be closing out your short position. Consequently, the capital gain resulting from the transaction is usually treated as a short-term gain.

Further complications arise if you have bought the underlying security before, after, or on the same day you bought the puts. The holding period treatment and other aspects of the transaction are affected in various ways that are not altogether cut and dried. Usually if you owned the underlying stock long-term before you bought the puts, the holding period will not be changed. If you owned the underlying stock short-term when you bought the puts, the holding period starts all over again when you sell the puts or they expire.

If you buy the puts the same day that you buy the underlying stock, and identify the puts as a hedge or insurance policy, the sale, exercise, or expiration of the puts will not affect the holding period of the stock. New puts that you acquire, however, will change the holding period of the underlying stock.

Since this area is so complex, I would strongly advise consulting a professional tax man for detailed advice, rather than attempting to unravel the tax ramifications yourself.

CALLS

When you buy calls and hold them until they expire, without exercising them, the premium you pay for them can be written off as a short-term loss for the year in which they expire. If you bought three KN 30 calls expiring in September of the current year for $400, and allow them to expire worthless, you have a $400 short-term loss for the year.

If the calls are sold before they expire, the resulting gain or loss is treated in the same fashion as a stock transaction, the same as with a gain or loss on puts. Again, your gain or loss on listed options will be short-term, since the maximum option life is nine months.

When you exercise your calls and buy the underlying stock at the strike price (buy 300 KN at $30 a share in the above example), the amount of premium you paid for the calls is added to the overall cost of your stock purchase. The holding period of the stock does *not* include the length of time you held the calls, and begins on the *day after* the calls are exercised.

Unlike the purchase of puts, the acquisition of calls is not regarded as a short sale for tax purposes. So, for short sale purposes, a call is not regarded as substantially the same as the underlying security. The holding period of the calls is not affected by shorting the underlying stock during the life of the options.

The holding period treatment resulting from the writing or selling of puts and calls is even more complicated than the situations already discussed. Generally speaking, the money you receive from the sale of puts and calls is regarded as ordinary income, but the holding period of the underlying stock is affected by whether you are writing covered or naked, when stock is put to you or called away, and other complex details.

Again, you will need the services of a tax professional to unravel the mystery and to interpret the tax laws when you are ready to square off against the IRS.

PART
III

12

My Latest Recommendations

Late April 1980 was an excellent time for buying stocks, following the breathtaking sell-off that started two months earlier. Those who bought the stocks I recommended in *The Optimist's Guide to Making Money in the 1980's,* and in my later book, *Mind Over Money,* and sold some shares as the DJIA advanced beyond 900, have already realized substantial profits.

The following stocks are my updated list of recommendations for the next buying opportunity. The next time the ATS tell you to buy stocks, select a few from the list and buy them when they fall within my recommended buying range. I have added new stocks to my earlier recommendations, removed a few and replaced them with others, and adjusted prices for splits, dividend increases, changes in earnings, and other pertinent data. Since this is a book and not a weekly market letter, some fundamentals may have changed by the time you read this. For the most part, however, you should make considerable profits if you buy and sell these stocks according to the dictates of the ATS.

When the DJIA is above 1050, stick to stocks with puts and calls that are listed in Chapter Ten.

Advertising

Company: JWT Group
Symbol: JWT
Exchange: NYSE
Dividend: Recent 25% stock
 dividend
EPS*: $2.88
Buying range: 20–22

Company: Doyle Dane Bernbach Intl.
Symbol: DOYL
Market: OTC
Dividend: $1.60
EPS: $4.60
Buying range: 23–25

*Earnings per share

Aerospace

Company: Boeing
Symbol: BA
Exchange: NYSE
Dividend: $1.50 plus extras
EPS: $6.00
Buying range: 30–32

Company: Northrop
Symbol: NOC
Exchange: NYSE
Dividend: $1.80
EPS: $5.50
Buying range: 30–32

Air Transport

Company: Northwest Airlines
Symbol: NWA
Exchange: NYSE
Dividend: $.80
EPS: $2.55
Buying range: 20–22

Appliance and TV

Company: RCA Corporation
Symbol: RCA
Exchange: NYSE
Dividend: $1.80
EPS: $3.60
Buying range: 20–23

Company: Hoover Co.
Symbol: HOOV
Market: OTC
Dividend: $1.00
EPS: $1.95
Buying range: 10–13

Company: Scovill Mfg.
Symbol: SCO
Exchange: NYSE
Dividend: $1.52
EPS: $3.20
Buying range: 16–18

Automotive: Car

Company: General Motors
Symbol: GM
Exchange: NYSE
Dividend: $4.00 plus extras
EPS: $5.00
Buying range: 40–43

Company: Ford Motor
Symbol: F
Exchange: NYSE
Dividend: $1.20
EPS: $3.00
Buying range: 21–23

Automotive: Diversified

Company: Eaton Corp.
Symbol: ETN
Exchange: NYSE
Dividend: $1.72 plus extras
EPS: $6.00
Buying range: 20–23

Company: Bendix Corp.
Symbol: BX
Exchange: NYSE
Dividend: $2.84
EPS: $6.80
Buying range: 36–40

Company: TRW, Inc.
Symbol: TRW
Exchange: NYSE
Dividend: $2.20
EPS: $6.10
Buying range: 30–34

Company: Borg-Warner
Symbol: BOR
Exchange: NYSE
Dividend: $2.30
EPS: $6.00
Buying range: 25–30

Automotive: Original Equipment

Company: Sheller-Globe
Symbol: SHG
Exchange: NYSE
Dividend: $.30
EPS: $1.00
Buying range: 5–7

Company: Arvin Industries
Symbol: ARV
Exchange: NYSE
Dividend: $1.12
EPS: $1.45
Buying range: 9–11

Automotive: Replacement Parts

Company: Allen Group
Symbol: ALN
Exchange: NYSE
Dividend: $1.00
EPS: $2.60
Buying range: 11–17

Automotive: Tire

Company: General Tire & Rubber
Symbol: GY
Exchange: NYSE
Dividend: $1.50
EPS: $1.70
Buying range: 12–14

Company: B. F. Goodrich
Symbol: GR
Exchange: NYSE
Dividend: $1.56
EPS: $3.35
Buying range: 16–19

Automotive: Truck

Company: Cummins Engine
Symbol: CUM
Exchange: NYSE
Dividend: $1.80
EPS: $7.50
Buying range: 28–32

Company: Freuhauf Corp.
Symbol: FTR
Exchange: NYSE
Dividend: $2.40
EPS: $4.35
Buying range: 22–26

Banks: Money Centered/International

Company: Continental Illinois
Symbol: CIL
Exchange: NYSE
Dividend: $1.60
EPS: $4.50
Buying range: 21–23

Company: J. P. Morgan & Co.
Symbol: JPM
Exchange: NYSE
Dividend: $2.80
EPS: $7.30
Buying range: 38–42

Company: First Chicago Corp.
Symbol: FNB
Exchange: NYSE
Dividend: $1.10
EPS: $2.50
Buying range: 10–12

Banks: Regional

Company: Mellon National Corp.
Symbol: MNBT
Market: OTC
Dividend: $1.84
EPS: $4.40
Buying range: 22–25

Company: Philadelphia National
Symbol: PHNA
Market: OTC
Dividend: $2.64
EPS: $4.91
Buying range: 24–28

Company: Chemical N.Y.
Symbol: CHL
Exchange: NYSE
Dividend: $3.48
EPS: $8.25
Buying range: 34–38

Beverages: Brewers

Company: Anheuser-Busch
Symbol: BUD
Market: NYSE
Dividend: $.96
EPS: $3.60
Buying range: 20–23

Beverages: Distillers

Company: Heublein
Symbol: HBL
Exchange: NYSE
Dividend: $1.66
EPS: $3.50
Buying range: 23–26

Beverages: Soft Drinks

Company: Royal Crown Cos.
Symbol: RCC
Exchange: NYSE
Dividend: $1.04
EPS: $1.50
Buying range: 10–12

Company: Coca-Cola Bott., N.Y.
Symbol: KNY
Exchange: NYSE
Dividend: $.16
EPS: $.45
Buying range: 4–5

Broadcasting

Company: American Broadcasting
  Co.
Symbol: ABC
Exchange: NYSE
Dividend: $1.60
EPS: $5.75
Buying range: 26–30

Company: Metromedia, Inc.
Symbol: MET
Exchange: NYSE
Dividend: $3.20
EPS: $10.80
Buying range: 55–60

Company: CBS, Inc.
Symbol: CBS
Exchange: NYSE
Dividend: $2.80
EPS: $7.10
Buying range: 40–44

Building Materials: Diversified

Company: Wickes Corp.
Symbol: WIX
Exchange: NYSE
Dividend: $1.04
EPS: $2.65
Buying range: 11–13

Company: Armstrong World
  Industries
Symbol: ACK
Exchange: NYSE
Dividend: $1.10
EPS: $2.75
Buying range: 12–14

Company: Johns-Mansville
Symbol: JM
Exchange: NYSE
Dividend: $1.92
EPS: $3.40
Buying range: 18–22

Building Materials: Retailers

No recommendations

Cable TV

Company: Satellite
  Communications
Symbol: SATV
Market: OTC
EPS: Not yet available
Buying range: 6-9

Canadian Financial Services

Company: Canadian Imperial
  Bank of Commerce
Symbol: CM
Exchange: Toronto, Montreal,
  Vancouver
Dividend: $1.80
EPS: $4.60
Buying range: 22–24

Company: Toronto-Dominion
  Bank
Symbol: TD
Exchange: Toronto, Montreal,
  Vancouver
Dividend: $1.36
EPS: $3.00
Buying range: 19–22

Canadian Mining

Company: Denison Mines Ltd.
Symbol: DENIF
Market: OTC
Dividend: $1.60
EPS: $4.00
Buying range: 20–25

Canadian Mining and Exploration

Company: Rio Algom Ltd.
Symbol: PRS
Exchange: ASE
Dividend: $1.50
EPS: $6.20
Buying range: 21–25

Canadian Oil Companies: Exploration

Company: Imperial Oil
Symbol: IMO.A
Exchange: ASE
Dividend: $1.40
EPS: $4.25
Buying range: 28–32

Canadian Oil Companies: Integrated

Company: Gulf Canada Ltd.
Symbol: GOC
Exchange: ASE
Dividend: Stock dividend plus
   extras
EPS: $3.91
Buying range: 22–25

Canadian Trust Companies

Company: Canada Trustco
   Mortgage Co.
Symbol: YCTA
Exchange: Toronto
Dividend: $1.32
EPS: $4.00
Buying range: 18–21

Chemicals: Diversified

Company: Akzona
Symbol: AXO
Exchange: NYSE
Dividend: $.80
EPS: $1.40
Buying range: 7–9

Company: Diamond Shamrock
Symbol: DIA
Exchange: NYSE
Dividend: $1.60
EPS: $4.00
Buying range: 22–25

Chemicals: Major

Company: duPont
Symbol: DD
Exchange: NYSE
Dividend: $2.00 plus extras
EPS: $6.00
Buying range: 31–34

Company: Union Carbide
Symbol: UK
Exchange: NYSE
Dividend: $3.20
EPS: $7.45
Buying range: 34–37

Company: Allied Chemical
Symbol: ACD
Exchange: NYSE
Dividend: $2.20
EPS: $7.20
Buying range: 32–36

Chemicals: Specialty

Company: Vulcan Materials
Symbol: VMC
Exchange: NYSE
Dividend: $2.00
EPS: $6.20
Buying range: 29–32

Company: Essex Chemicals
Symbol: ESX
Exchange: NYSE
Dividend: $.80
EPS: $1.70
Buying range: 9–12

Coal

Company: Pittston
Symbol: PCO
Exchange: NYSE
Dividend: $1.20
EPS: $1.10 (should improve
    substantially over long term)
Buying range: 16–20

Communications

Company: American Tel & Tel
Symbol: T
Exchange: NYSE
Dividend: $5.00
EPS: $7.75
Buying range: 45–50

Company: New England Tel & Tel
Symbol: NTT
Exchange: NYSE
Dividend: $3.40
EPS: $4.25
Buying range: 28–32

Company: General Telephone &
  Electronics
Symbol: GTE
Exchange: NYSE
Dividend: $2.72
EPS: $3.40
Buying range: 23–26

Conglomerates

Company: Northwest Industries
Symbol: NWT
Exchange: NYSE
Dividend: $2.28
EPS: $5.00
Buying range: 23–26

Company: Martin Marietta
Symbol: ML
Exchange: NYSE
Dividend: $2.32
EPS: $7.40
Buying range: 35–39

Company: Ogden Corp.
Symbol: OG
Exchange: NYSE
Dividend: $2.20
EPS: $7.00
Buying range: 27–30

Construction Contractors

Company: Stone & Webster
Symbol: SW
Exchange: NYSE
Dividend: $2.75
EPS: $7.00
Buying range: 40–44

Containers: Glass

Company: Anchor Hocking
Symbol: ARH
Exchange: NYSE
Dividend: $1.28
EPS: $2.65
Buying range: 13–15

Company: Owens-Illinois
Symbol: OI
Exchange: NYSE
Dividend: $1.40
EPS: $4.80
Buying range: 18–21

Containers: Metals

Company: American Can
Symbol: AC
Exchange: NYSE
Dividend: $2.90
EPS: $5.30
Buying range: 27–30

Company: Continental Group
Symbol: CCC
Exchange: NYSE
Dividend: $2.40
EPS: $5.00
Buying range: 24–27

Cosmetics and Toiletries

Company: Avon Products
Symbol: AVP
Exchange: NYSE
Dividend: $3.00
EPS: $3.95
Buying range: 31–34

Company: Gillette
Symbol: GS
Exchange: NYSE
Dividend: $1.90
EPS: $3.90
Buying range: 17–21

Drugs

Company: American Home
   Products
Symbol: AHP
Exchange: NYSE
Dividend: $1.70
EPS: $2.60
Buying range: 21–24

Company: Squibb Corp.
Symbol: SQB
Exchange: NYSE
Dividend: $1.14
EPS: $2.60
Buying range: 19–23

Electrical Equipment

Company: Gould
Symbol: GLD
Exchange: NYSE
Dividend: $1.72
EPS: $3.50
Buying range: 19–22

Electrical Equipment: Major Diversified

Company: Westinghouse Electric
Symbol: WX
Exchange: NYSE
Dividend: $1.40
EPS: $3.85
Buying range: 18–22

Company: General Electric
Symbol: GE
Exchange: NYSE
Dividend: $3.00
EPS: $6.35
Buying range: 42–46

Electronics: Instrumentation

Company: Perkin-Elmer
Symbol: PKN
Exchange: NYSE
Dividend: $.72 (low yield, but
  good chance for dividend
  increase)
EPS: $3.30
Buying range: 26–30

Electronics: Semiconductor/Components

Company: Avnet
Symbol: AVT
Exchange: NYSE
Dividend: $1.00
EPS: $4.60
Buying range: 18–22

Company: Texas Instruments
Symbol: TXN
Exchange: NYSE
Dividend: $2.00
EPS: $7.75
Buying range: 75–80

Entertainment

No recommendations

Fertilizers

Company: Williams Cos.
Symbol: WMB
Exchange: NYSE
Dividend: $1.10
EPS: $3.50
Buying range: 19–23

Finance

Company: Beneficial Corp.
Symbol: BNL
Exchange: NYSE
Dividend: $2.00
EPS: $3.85
Buying range: 18–21

Company: Household Finance
Symbol: HFC
Exchange: NYSE
Dividend: $1.55
EPS: $3.20
Buying range: 14–17

Foods: Bakers

Company: Campbell Taggart
Symbol: CTI
Exchange: NYSE
Dividend: $1.20
EPS: $3.10
Buying range: 19–21

Foods: Canned

Company: H. J. Heinz
Symbol: HNZ
Exchange: NYSE
Dividend: $2.20
EPS: $6.25
Buying range: 33–36

Company: Campbell Soup
Symbol: CPB
Exchange: NYSE
Dividend: $1.90
EPS: $4.20
Buying range: 24–27

Foods: Commodities

Company: Alexander & Baldwin
Symbol: ALEX
Market: OTC
Dividend: $1.60
EPS: $4.75
Buying range: 19–23

Company: A. E. Staley
Symbol: STA
Exchange: NYSE
Dividend: $1.00
EPS: $3.50
Buying range: 22–26

Foods: Confectionery

Company: Russell Stover Candies
Symbol: RUSS
Market: OTC
Dividend: $.90
EPS: $1.67
Buying range: 11–13

Foods: Dairy Products

Company: Borden, Inc.
Symbol: BN
Exchange: NYSE
Dividend: $1.90
EPS: $4.30
Buying range: 19–23

Company: Kraft, Inc.
Symbol: KRA
Exchange: NYSE
Dividend: $3.20
EPS: $7.20
Buying range: 38–42

Foods: Meat Packing

Company: Esmark
Symbol: ESM
Exchange: NYSE
Dividend: $1.84
EPS: $4.40
Buying range: 22–26

Company: Oscar Mayer & Co.
Symbol: OMC
Exchange: NYSE
Dividend: $1.10
EPS: $2.80
Buying range: 15–17

Foods: Processed

Company: Kellogg Co.
Symbol: K
Exchange: NYSE
Dividend: $1.32
EPS: $1.90
Buying range: 15–18

Company: Standard Brands
Symbol: SB
Exchange: NYSE
Dividend: $1.64
EPS: $3.10
Buying range: 21–24

Company: General Foods
Symbol: GF
Exchange: NYSE
Dividend: $2.20
EPS: $4.90
Buying range: 23–26

Company: Ralston Purina
Symbol: RAL
Exchange: NYSE
Dividend: $.64
EPS: $1.40
Buying range: 9–11

Foreign: European

Company: Rank Org.
Symbol: RANKY
Market: OTC
Dividend: $.21
EPS: $.70
Buying range: 2¾–3½

Foreign: Japanese

No recommendations

Foreign: South African

Company: Precious Metals
Symbol: PMH
Exchange: ASE
Dividend: $1.36
NAV: $24
Buying range: 20–25

Forest Products

Company: Georgia-Pacific
Symbol: GP
Exchange: NYSE
Dividend: $1.20
EPS: $2.40
Buying range: 20–22

Company: Weyerhaeuser Co.
Symbol: WY
Exchange: NYSE
Dividend: $1.30
EPS: $3.60
Buying range: 25–29

Home Builders

No recommendations

Home Furnishings

Company: Interco, Inc.
Symbol: ISS
Market: NYSE
Dividend: $2.64
EPS: $7.50
Buying range: 35–40

Company: Shaw Industries
Symbol: SHX
Exchange: ASE
Dividend: $.30
EPS: $.90
Buying range: 4–5

Hospital Management

No recommendations

Hospital Supplies

Company: Abbott Laboratories
Symbol: ABT
Exchange: NYSE
Dividend: $1.20
EPS: $3.20
Buying range: 23–26

Company: Angelica Corp.
Symbol: AGL
Exchange: NYSE
Dividend: $.40
EPS: $1.15
Buying range: 5–7

Household Products

Company: Clorox Co.
Symbol: CLX
Exchange: NYSE
Dividend: $.80
EPS: $1.63
Buying range: 8–10

Company: Colgate-Palmolive
Symbol: CL
Exchange: NYSE
Dividend: $1.08
EPS: $2.15
Buying range: 11–13

Housewares

Company: Lenox
Symbol: LNX
Exchange: NYSE
Dividend: $1.48
EPS: $3.70
Buying range: 21–24

Company: Mirro Aluminum
Symbol: MIR
Exchange: NYSE
Dividend: $.96
EPS: $1.39
Buying range: 9–10

Insurance: Casualty

Company: Chubb Corp.
Symbol: CHUB
Market: OTC
Dividend: $2.40
EPS: $6.95
Buying range: 30–34

Company: U.S. Fidelity &
 Guaranty
Symbol: FG
Exchange: NYSE
Dividend: $7.80
EPS: $6.75
Buying range: 33–36

Company: Crum & Forster
Symbol: CMF
Exchange: NYSE
Dividend: Recent split plus extras
EPS: $5.10
Buying range: 25–27

Insurance: Multiline

Company: Aetna Life & Casualty
Symbol: AET
Exchange: NYSE
Dividend: $2.12
EPS: $6.85
Buying range: 29–32

Insurance: Specialty

Company: American Express
Symbol: AXP
Exchange: NYSE
Dividend: $2.00
EPS: $4.20
Buying range: 25–28

Company: American Family
Symbol: AFL
Exchange: NYSE
Dividend: $.60 plus extras
EPS: $2.00
Buying range: 7–9

Leisure Time

Company: Brunswick Corp.
Symbol: BC
Exchange: NYSE
Dividend: $.90
EPS: $1.40
Buying range: 10–12

Company: Outboard Marine
Symbol: OM
Exchange: NYSE
Dividend: $.70
EPS: $.28 (depressed earnings that
    should be reversed)
Buying range: 9–11

Lodging

Company: Holiday Inns
Symbol: HIA
Exchange: NYSE
Dividend: $.70
EPS: $2.75
Buying range: 12–15

Company: Hilton Hotels
Symbol: HLT
Exchange: NYSE
Dividend: $1.36
EPS: $3.60
Buying range: 25–28

Machinery: Agricultural

Company: Deere & Co.
Symbol: DE
Exchange: NYSE
Dividend: $1.90
EPS: $4.85
Buying range: 28–32

Company: International Harvester
Symbol: HR
Exchange: NYSE
Dividend: $2.50
EPS: $4.75
Buying range: 23–26

Machinery: Agricultural (*continued*)

Company: Allis-Chalmers
Symbol: AH
Exchange: NYSE
Dividend: $2.00
EPS: $4.50
Buying range: 22–25

Machinery: Construction and Material Handling

Company: American Hoist &
  Derrick
Symbol: AHO
Exchange: NYSE
Dividend: $1.12
EPS: $3.55
Buying range: 13–16

Company: Clark Equipment
Symbol: CKL
Exchange: NYSE
Dividend: $2.20
EPS: $6.00
Buying range: 28–32

Machinery: Industrial

Company: Cooper Industries
Symbol: CBE
Exchange: NYSE
Dividend: Recent split plus extras
EPS: $4.00
Buying range: 30–34

Company: Joy Manufacturing
Symbol: JOY
Exchange: NYSE
Dividend: $1.90
EPS: $4.45
Buying range: 25–29

Company: Ingersoll-Rand
Symbol: IR
Exchange: NYSE
Dividend: $3.32
EPS: $6.70
Buying range: 45–49

Machinery: Specialty

Company: Black & Decker Mfg.
Symbol: BDK
Exchange: NYSE
Dividend: $.76
EPS: $3.20
Buying range: 17–19

Company: Ex-Cell-O Corp.
Symbol: XLO
Exchange: NYSE
Dividend: $2.00
EPS: $6.00
Buying range: 26–30

Medical: Specialty

Company: Sybron Corp.
Symbol: SYB
Exchange: NYSE
Dividend: $1.08
EPS: $2.50
Buying range: 12–14

Merchandising: Department

Company: Allied Stores
Symbol: ALS
Exchange: NYSE
Dividend: $1.70
EPS: $3.75
Buying range: 18–20

Company: Marshall Field
Symbol: MF
Exchange: NYSE
Dividend: $1.24
EPS: $1.60
Buying range: 12–15

Company: Murphy (G. C.)
Symbol: MPH
Exchange: NYSE
Dividend: $1.28
EPS: $2.95
Buying range: 12–14

Merchandising: Drug

Company: Walgreen Co.
Symbol: WAG
Exchange: NYSE
Dividend: $1.60
EPS: $5.00
Buying range: 24–27

Merchandising: Food

Company: Safeway Stores
Symbol: SA
Exchange: NYSE
Dividend: $2.60
EPS: $5.25
Buying range: 26–30

Company: Wetterau
Symbol: WETT
Market: OTC
Dividend: $.70 plus extras
EPS: $1.64
Buying range: 9–11

Merchandising: Mass

Company: Penney (J. C.)
Symbol: JCP
Exchange: NYSE
Dividend: $1.84
EPS: $3.25
Buying range: 19–22

Company: Sears, Roebuck & Co.
Symbol: S
Exchange: NYSE
Dividend: $1.36
EPS: $1.85 (should improve long term)
Buying range: 15–18

Merchandising: Specialty

Company: Lane Bryant
Symbol: LNY
Exchange: NYSE
Dividend: $1.00
EPS: $2.18
Buying range: 11–13

Company: Zale Corp.
Symbol: ZAL
Exchange: NYSE
Dividend: $1.08
EPS: $4.00
Buying range: 15–18

Metals: Aluminum

Company: Alcan Aluminum Ltd.
Symbol: AL
Exchange: NYSE
Dividend: $1.40 plus extras
EPS: $1.65 (should improve near term)
Buying range: 20–23

Company: Reynolds Metals
Symbol: RLM
Exchange: NYSE
Dividend: $2.20
EPS: $7.70
Buying range: 26–30

Metals: Copper

Company: Kennecott
Symbol: KN
Exchange: NYSE
Dividend: $1.40
EPS: $5.10
Buying range: 22–25

Metals: Diversified Mining

Company: Cleveland-Cliffs Iron
Symbol: CLF
Exchange: NYSE
Dividend: $1.40 plus extras
EPS: $4.35
Buying range: 25–28

Company: Texasgulf
Symbol: TG
Exchange: NYSE
Dividend: $1.60
EPS: $5.50
Buying range: 27–32

Metals: Diversified Mining (*continued*)

Company: Amax
Symbol: AMX
Exchange: NYSE
Dividend: $2.40
EPS: $8.50
Buying range: 35–40

Metals: Miscellaneous

Company: GK Technology
   (formerly General Cable)
Symbol: GK
Exchange: NYSE
Dividend: $1.50
EPS: $5.50
Buying range: 17–22

Company: Crane Co.
Symbol: CR
Exchange: NYSE
Dividend: $1.60 plus extras
EPS: $5.00
Buying range: 27–31

Metals: Specialty Steel

Company: Allegheny Ludlum
Symbol: AG
Exchange: NYSE
Dividend: $1.40
EPS: $7.50
Buying range: 19–23

Company: Carpenter Technology
Symbol: CRS
Exchange: NYSE
Dividend: $1.90
EPS: $4.80
Buying range: 24–27

Metals: Steel

Company: U.S. Steel
Symbol: X
Exchange: NYSE
Dividend: $1.60 (in danger of
   being cut)
EPS: Showing a loss, but should
   improve long term
Buying range: 15–18

Company: Bethlehem Steel
Symbol: BS
Exchange: NYSE
Dividend: $1.60
EPS: $4.75
Buying range: 18–22

Miscellaneous

Company: PPG Industries
Symbol: PPG
Exchange: NYSE
Dividend: $2.16
EPS: $5.50
Buying range: 25–28

Company: White Consolidated
   Industries
Symbol: WSW
Exchange: NYSE
Dividend: $1.40
EPS: $4.90
Buying range: 19–21

Miscellaneous (*continued*)

Company: Occidental Petroleum
Symbol: OXY
Exchange: NYSE
Dividend: $2.00
EPS: $8.30
Buying range: 19–22

Mobile Homes

Company: Skyline Corp.
Symbol: SKY
Exchange: NYSE
Dividend: $.48
EPS: $.54 (should improve near term)
Buying range: 8–11

Company: Philips Industries
Symbol: PHL
Exchange: NYSE
Dividend: $.32
EPS: $1.15
Buying range: 4–5

Office Equipment: Computer

Company: IBM
Symbol: IBM
Exchange: NYSE
Dividend: $3.44
EPS: $5.30
Buying range: 50–55

Company: Honeywell
Symbol: HON
Exchange: NYSE
Dividend: $3.00
EPS: $10.80
Buying range: 65–70

Company: Sperry Rand
Symbol: SY
Exchange: NYSE
Dividend: $1.76
EPS: $7.50
Buying range: 40–44

Office Equipment: Copying

Company: Xerox Corp.
Symbol: XRX
Exchange: NYSE
Dividend: $2.80
EPS: $7.10
Buying range: 46–50

Company: Savin Corp.
Symbol: SVB
Exchange: NYSE
Dividend: $.70
EPS: $4.60
Buying range: 12–14

Office Equipment: Miscellaneous

Company: Dennison Mfg.
Symbol: DSN
Exchange: NYSE
Dividend: $1.16
EPS: $2.40
Buying range: 14–16

Oil and Gas Producers

Company: Houston Oil & Mineral
($1.69 cumulative convertible
preferred)
Symbol: HOI Pr A
Exchange: AMEX
Dividend: $1.69
EPS: $2.35 (convertible into .833
shares of common)
Buying range: 17–20

Company: Louisiana Land and
Exploration
Symbol: LLX
Exchange: NYSE
Dividend: $1.80
EPS: $4.60
Buying range: 28–32

Oil: Integrated Domestic

Company: Atlantic Richfield
Symbol: ARC
Exchange: NYSE
Dividend: Recent split plus extras
EPS: $5.20
Buying range: 40–43

Company: Standard Oil of Indiana
Symbol: SN
Exchange: NYSE
Dividend: $2.20 (recent split plus
extras)
EPS: $6.50
Buying range: 45–49

Company: Amerada Hess
Symbol: AHC
Exchange: NYSE
Dividend: $2.00 (plus stock
dividend)
EPS: $12.00
Buying range: 35–40 (split
pending)

Company: Shell Oil
Symbol: SUO
Exchange: NYSE
Dividend: Recent stock dividend
plus extras
EPS: $4.15
Buying range: 28–32

Company: Conoco
Symbol: CLL
Exchange: NYSE
Dividend: $2.20
EPS: $9.50
Buying range: 35–40

Oil: Integrated International

Company: Mobil Corp.
Symbol: MOB
Exchange: NYSE
Dividend: $3.40
EPS: $13.00
Buying range: 45–50

Company: Gulf Oil
Symbol: GO
Exchange: NYSE
Dividend: $2.50
EPS: $8.60
Buying range: 27–32

Company: Exxon Corp.
Symbol: XON
Exchange: NYSE
Dividend: $5.20
EPS: $11.60
Buying range: 52–56

Company: Texaco, Inc.
Symbol: TX
Exchange: NYSE
Dividend: $2.40
EPS: $7.40
Buying range: 28–32

Oil Services: Drilling

Company: Reading and Bates
Symbol: RB
Exchange: NYSE
Dividend: $.80 (recent stock
   dividend plus extras)
EPS: $4.35
Buying range: 25–29

Oil Services: Products

Company: Philadelphia Suburban
Symbol: PSC
Exchange: NYSE
Dividend: $1.24
EPS: $3.20
Buying range: 22–26

Company: NL Industries
Symbol: NL
Exchange: NYSE
Dividend: $1.20
EPS: $4.10
Buying range: 24–28

Company: J. Ray McDermott
Symbol: MDE
Exchange: NYSE
Dividend: $1.40.
EPS: $4.10
Buying range: 19–23

Paper Products

Company: Hammermill Paper
Symbol: HML
Exchange: NYSE
Dividend: $1.50
EPS: $5.20
Buying range: 17–20

Company: Kimberly-Clark
Symbol: KMB
Exchange: NYSE
Dividend: $3.20
EPS: $6.70
Buying range: 36–40

Company: St. Regis Paper
Symbol: SRT
Exchange: NYSE
Dividend: $2.00
EPS: $5.10
Buying range: 24–27

Company: Scott Paper
Symbol: SPP
Exchange: NYSE
Dividend: $1.00
EPS: $3.80
Buying range: 13–16

Photography

Company: Polaroid
Symbol: PRD
Exchange: NYSE
Dividend: $1.00
EPS: $1.20 (depressed earnings
  should improve dramatically)
Buying range: 19–23

Company: Eastman Kodak
Symbol: EK
Exchange: NYSE
Dividend: $2.40 (plus extras)
EPS: $6.60
Buying range: 42–46

Pollution Control

Company: Wheelabrator-Frye
Symbol: WFI
Exchange: NYSE
Dividend: $1.40
EPS: $4.00
Buying range: 26–31

Company: Zurn Industries
Symbol: ZRN
Exchange: NYSE
Dividend: $.92
EPS: $2.70
Buying range: 13–16

Printing

Company: R. R. Donnelly & Sons
Symbol: DNY
Exchange: NYSE
Dividend: $1.14
EPS: $3.70
Buying range: 22–25

Publishing: Books

Company: Prentice-Hall
Symbol: PTN
Exchange: AMEX
Dividend: $1.48
EPS: $2.80
Buying range: 16–19

Company: Macmillan
Symbol: MLL
Exchange: NYSE
Dividend: $.82
EPS: $.94 (should improve near
    term)
Buying range: 10–12

Company: McGraw-Hill
Symbol: MHP
Exchange: NYSE
Dividend: $1.52
EPS: $3.15
Buying range: 23–26

Publishing: Newspapers

Company: Times Mirror Co.
Symbol: TMC
Exchange: NYSE
Dividend: $1.44
EPS: $4.15
Buying range: 28–32

Company: Gannett Co.
Symbol: GCI
Exchange: NYSE
Dividend: $2.00
EPS: $3.80
Buying range: 38–42

Publishing: Printing Miscellaneous

Company: American Greetings,
    Class A
Symbol: AGREA
Market: OTC
Dividend: $.52
EPS: $1.85
Buying range: 8–10

Company: Dun and Bradstreet
    Cos.
Symbol: DNB
Exchange: NYSE
Dividend: $2.04
EPS: $3.30
Buying range: 31–35

Railroads

Company: Santa Fe Industries
Symbol: SFF
Exchange: NYSE
Dividend: $2.60
EPS: $8.25
Buying range: 40–45

Company: Union Pacific
Symbol: UNP
Exchange: NYSE
Dividend: $1.40 (recent split plus
    extras)
EPS: $4.25
Buying range: 25–30

Railroad Equipment

Company: GATX Corp.
Symbol: GMT
Exchange: NYSE
Dividend: $2.20
EPS: $4.75
Buying range: 23–26

Company: Pullman
Symbol: PU
Exchange: NYSE
Dividend: $1.00
EPS: $6.00
Buying range: 20–23

Real Estate

Company: Connecticut General
    Mortgage & Realty
Symbol: CGM
Exchange: NYSE
Dividend: $2.00
EPS: $1.46 (equity/share: $20.00)
Buying range: 17–20

Company: Lomas & Nettleton
    Financial
Symbol: LNF
Exchange: NYSE
Dividend: $1.00
EPS: $2.30 (equity/share: $12.21)
Buying range: 9–12

Company: Wells Fargo Mortgage
    and Equity Trust
Symbol: WFM
Exchange: NYSE
Dividend: $1.40
EPS: $2.10 (equity/share: $18.46
Buying range: 11–14

Company: Lomas & Nettleton
    Mortgage Inv.
Symbol: LOM
Exchange: NYSE
Dividend: $2.20
EPS: $2.40 (equity/share: $27.91)
Buying range: 14–18

Company: Hubbard Real Estate
    Inv.
Symbol: HRE
Exchange: NYSE
Dividend: $1.76
EPS: $1.85
Buying range: 13–15

Company: MGIC Investment
    Corp.
Symbol: MGI
Exchange: NYSE
Dividend: $1.12
EPS: $3.40
Buying range: 16–19

Restaurants

Company: Chart House
Symbol: CHHO
Market: OTC
Dividend: $1.04
EPS: $3.30
Buying range: 13–16

Savings and Loan

Company: Great Western
   Financial
Symbol: GWF
Exchange: NYSE
Dividend: $.88
EPS: $3.70
Buying range: 14–17

Services

Company: Saga Corp.
Symbol: SGA
Exchange: NYSE
Dividend: $.44
EPS: $.71
Buying range: 5–7

Shoes

Company: U.S. Shoe
Symbol: USR
Exchange: NYSE
Dividend: $1.60
EPS: $4.50
Buying range: 16–19

Textile: Apparel

Company: West Point-Pepperell
Symbol: WPM
Exchange: NYSE
Dividend: $3.20
EPS: $8.00
Buying range: 27–31

Company: Palm Beach
Symbol: PMB
Exchange: NYSE
Dividend: $1.20
EPS: $3.00
Buying range: 13–15

Company: Levi Strauss
Symbol: LVI
Exchange: NYSE
Dividend: $1.10 (recent stock
   split)
EPS: $5.00
Buying range: 28–32

Textile: Products

Company: Collins and Aikman
Symbol: CK
Exchange: NYSE
Dividend: $.72
EPS: $1.17 (should improve long
 term)
Buying range: 5–7

Company: Burlington Industries
Symbol: BUR
Exchange: NYSE
Dividend: $1.40
EPS: $2.80
Buying range: 14–17

Tobacco

Company: R. J. Reynolds
 Industries
Symbol: RJR
Exchange: NYSE
Dividend: $2.10
EPS: $5.60
Buying range: 27–31

Toys

Company: Mattel
Symbol: MAT
Exchange: NYSE
Dividend: $.30
EPS: $1.25
Buying range: 6–7

Transportation: Miscellaneous

Company: Transway International
Symbol: TNW
Exchange: NYSE
Dividend: $1.80
EPS: $3.50
Buying range: 19–21

Truckers

Company: Consolidated
 Freightways
Symbol: CNF
Exchange: NYSE
Dividend: $1.40
EPS: $4.80
Buying range: 18–20

Company: McLean Trucking
Symbol: MLN
Exchange: NYSE
Dividend: $.64
EPS: Deficit, but should improve
 near term
Buying range: 6–8

Utilities: Electric

Electric utilities are bought primarily for income rather than for growth. When selecting utilities for your income portfolio, try to time your purchases when interest rates are relatively high. Most of the time utility stocks behave more like bonds and other fixed-income securities than like other common stocks. When interest rates start to decline, utility stocks generally rise in value and vice versa. Concentrate on those with a good history of dividend increases and tax-deferred treatment of the dividends. Some major electric utilities that meet both these criteria are:

American Electric Power
  Current yield: 11%
  Current tax deferment: 32%

Dayton Power & Light
  Current yield: 11.8%
  Current tax deferment: 70%

San Diego Gas & Electric
  Current yield: 11.5%
  Current tax deferment: 100%

N.Y. State Electric & Gas
  Current yield: 10.7%
  Current tax deferment: 10%

Portland General Electric
  Current yield: 11.7%
  Current tax deferment: 100%

Niagara Mohawk
  Current yield: 11.1%
  Current tax deferment: 65%

Long Island Lighting
  Current yield: 11.5%
  Current tax deferment: 100%

Philadelphia Electric
  Current yield: 12.5%
  Current tax deferment: 100%

Ohio Edison
  Current yield: 11.7%
  Current tax deferment: 72%

Pennsylvania Power & Light
  Current yield: 10.5%
  Current tax deferment: 50%

Cleveland Electric Illuminating
  Current yield: 11.4%
  Current tax deferment: 44%

Public Service Electric & Gas
  Current yield: 11.1%
  Current tax deferment: 40%

Columbus & Southern Ohio
  Current yield: 10.2%
  Current tax deferment: 40%

Utilities: Gas Distribution

Company: Arkansas Louisiana Gas Co.
Symbol: ALG
Exchange: NYSE
Dividend: $1.24
EPS: $2.90
Buying range: 19–23

Company: Pioneer Corp.
Symbol: PNA
Exchange: NYSE
Dividend: $1.40
EPS: $4.00
Buying range: 24–29

Utilities: Gas Distribution (*continued*)

Company: Columbia Gas System
Symbol: CG
Exchange: NYSE
Dividend: $2.56
EPS: $4.10
Buying range: 26–30

Utilities: Gas Pipeline

Company: El Paso Co.
Symbol: ELG
Exchange: NYSE
Dividend: $1.48
EPS: $3.00
Buying range: 15–18

Company: Texas Gas Transmission
Symbol: TXG
Exchange: NYSE
Dividend: $1.46
EPS: $4.15
Buying range: 21–25

Company: Tenneco
Symbol: TGT
Exchange: NYSE
Dividend: $2.40
EPS: $5.70
Buying range: 28–32

Company: Nicor, Inc.
Symbol: GAS
Exchange: NYSE
Dividend: $2.68
EPS: $4.50
Buying range: 26–29

A Glossary of Terms Used in Tax Shelters

Reading a prospectus can be a nerve-wracking experience if you are not familiar with the terminology commonly used in tax shelters. A tax shelter prospectus can be an impenetrable verbal jungle. Such language is, of course, the stuff that puts meat and potatoes on the tables of lawyers and accountants, and you should utilize the service of one of these professionals before committing your dollars to any shelter program. However, you should also have a passing acquaintance with the basic terminology so that you at least have a vague notion of what the professionals are talking about when they get into the details of a tax shelter program. The following will help to clear up some of the mystery.

Accelerated Depreciation

An optional type of depreciation deduction (see below) that permits recovery of a greater percentage of the capitalized costs of an asset during the early years of the asset's useful life than would be recovered under the straight-line method. The declining balance method and the sum-of-the-years'-digits method are commonly applied forms of accelerated depreciation.

Assessment

Additional amounts of capital that a limited partner in a tax shelter may be required to furnish beyond his original investment. A given program, depending on the terms of the agreement, may be either assessable or nonassessable.

Capital Asset

Any asset, as defined by the tax laws, that is not purchased or held for use in a trade or business and, therefore, is subject to a capital gains tax if it is sold for a profit, or is deductible as a capital loss if sold for a loss.

Capital Gain or Loss

Profit or loss resulting from the sale or exchange of a capital asset. A capital asset must be held for a year and a day to qualify for long-term tax treatment of the gain, which currently is a maximum of 28 percent of the total profit. A capital loss must be short-term for it to be fully deductible.

Capitalized Costs

Costs that, for tax purposes, must be recovered through depreciation over a period of years, as opposed to costs that are granted an immediate tax deduction.

Cash Liquidating Value

The amount, usually based on an evaluation by a qualified appraiser, that will be paid to a limited partner for his interest in a tax shelter by the sponsor of the program. Not all tax shelter programs offer this kind of liquidity. It is important to read the prospectus and offering agreement carefully to find out exactly what kind of a program you are getting into.

Deduction

Anything that allows you to reduce your taxable income and lower the amount of taxes you have to pay. Expenses incurred in a business operation are allowable as deductions. In a tax shelter program, however, the limited partner is ordinarily offered extremely high deductions, which is the main reason for investing in a shelter in the first place. In an oil and gas shelter, the intangible drilling costs are the primary source of deductions, while in a real estate program depreciation and interest are the primary deductions.

Deferral

While deductions are allowed immediately, during the limited partner's high-income years, a tax deferral postpones capital gains and income taxes to later years when the limited partner is either retired or in a lower income bracket.

Depletion

A tax deduction permitting tax-free recovery of the costs of exploration and development of oil and gas in order to encourage the development of new energy supplies. Depletion is similar to depreciation (see below) except that depletion is available as long as there is income from the gas or oil well, while depreciation stops after the initial costs are recovered.

Depreciation

A tax deduction designed to permit recovery of all or part of the capitalized costs from the income generated by a shelter program. Current tax laws permit either straight-line depreciation, which remains constant over the life of the program, or one of several types of accelerated depreciation.

Developmental Program

The safest kind of oil and gas shelters. Developmental drilling takes place in an area where the presence of hydrocarbons has already been indicated. The success ratio of developmental drilling is three to four times as great as that of exploratory drilling. Since the element of risk is reduced, a developmental program does not offer as great a tax write-off as an exploratory program does, but the economic reward in terms of income from producing wells is usually greater.

Exploratory Program

The highest degree of risk in an oil and gas shelter. The drilling is done in areas where oil and gas have not previously been found. The tax write-off in an exploratory program is far greater than that in a developmental program, since the economic success ratio is lower. However, a highly successful exploratory program can produce tremendous returns for those who don't mind assuming the extra risk.

General Partner

The sponsor of a tax shelter program; the manager, operator, or management company that provides its expertise to attempt to make the program a successful one. The general partner or sponsor may or may not have his own money invested in the venture. The prospectus or offering agreement will spell this out in detail.

Intangible Drilling Costs

Expenditures incurred in the drilling and completion of oil and gas wells that are granted a deduction from current income for tax purposes. Intangibles are the items that have no salvage value, such as labor, chemicals, and drill-site preparation. They usually amount to between 50 and 70 percent of the cost of drilling and completing a well.

Investment Tax Credit

A tax credit, usually equal to 10 percent of the cost of so-called qualified personal property. Qualified personal property includes items used in tax shelters that are depreciable and have useful lives of three years or longer.

Limited Partner

A participant in a tax shelter program. The limited partners put up all or most of the money needed to run the program, but their liability in the case of failure or bankruptcy is limited to the amount of their investment. The general partner is fully responsible for all claims against the business. In return for his investment, the limited partner receives a deduction on his taxable income, and he also shares in any profits the program generates.

Noncash Charges

A term that refers to depreciation and depletion. These are deductions subtracted from gross income in calculating taxable income that do not involve actual payments. Noncash charges reduce taxable income without reducing spendable cash. Some tax shelter programs generate noncash deductions that completely or partially offset taxable income and still have money available for distribution to the limited partners. When this is available, these funds are referred to as tax-sheltered cash flow.

Organization and Offering Expenses

Those expenses incurred in the preparation of a public tax shelter program (see below) for registration with the Securites Exchange Commission, and in offering and distributing it to the public. These expenses include sales commissions that are paid to broker-dealers who sell the shelter to their customers.

Overcall

The same thing as an *assessment*.

Participant

An investor in a tax shelter program. Most shelters are organized as limited partnerships, but some are not.

Private Program

A tax shelter program that is not registered with the Securities Exchange Commission. Instead it is offered and sold under an exemption from registration granted by the Securities Act of 1933 or by the securities regulation authorities of various states.

Public Program

A tax shelter program that is registered with the Securities Exchange Commission and is distributed to the public by the general partner or sponsor himself, or by various broker-dealers. Most public programs are organized as limited partnerships.

Recapture

When a capital asset is sold on which certain deductions have been claimed, parts of the gain must be added to taxable income in the year the gain is taken; some of these gains are taxed as ordinary income, while the remainder are taxed as capital gains. Deductions that are ordinarily subject to recapture include the excess of accelerated depreciation over straight-line depreciation, and the excess of intangible drilling costs over the amount that would have been deducted had the well been claimed as a capital asset and depreciated over the useful life of the well. In effect, the government is recapturing part of the earlier deductions and taxing them when an asset is sold.

Sponsor

The same as the *general partner,* manager, or management company.

Subscription

The total dollar amount that a participant in a tax shelter program agrees to invest. It does not include any additional sum, such as an assessment, that he has the option to reject.

Tax (Minimum, Alternative Minimum, Maximum)

Minimum tax on tax preference items was created by Congress to make sure that all taxpayers pay at least some taxes. The minimum taxes in tax shelter programs are:
    1. Intangible drilling expenses incurred on oil and gas wells;
    2. Percentage depletion that exceeds your adjusted basis in an oil and gas well;

3. Accelerated depreciation above straight line on personal property subject to lease;

4. Accelerated depreciation above straight line on real property;

5. Itemized deductions, other than medical and casualty loss, in excess of 60 percent of adjusted gross income.

The *alternative minimum tax* applies to individual taxpayers who have significant capital gains or excess itemized deduction preference items. It is not an add-on tax, but rather an alternative method of calculating minimum tax.

Maximum tax levied on personal service income, such as wages, salary, professional fees, and certain income from pensions, annuities, and deferred compensation, is limited to 50 percent. The amount of income subject to maximum tax can be reduced dollar for dollar by the sum of a taxpayer's items of tax preference. The balance is taxed at unearned income tax rates.

Tax Shelter Programs

An investment program offering the participant a combination of economic profit and favorable tax treatment. Characteristics usually include:

1. Capital gains opportunities;
2. High deductions;
3. Deferral of income;
4. Depletion;
5. Accelerated depreciation.

The flow-through of tax benefits is usually the main feature of a shelter program, regardless of the industry represented or the way the program is distributed. The program is created for the mutual benefit of the sponsor and the participants. It can be structured as a limited partnership, a joint venture, or sometimes as a Sub-Chapter S corporation. It may either be a public or a private program.

Tax-sheltered Cash Flow

The same as *noncash charges*.

Write-off

A nontechnical term for tax *deduction*.